OVERCOMING ANXIETY GOD'S WAY

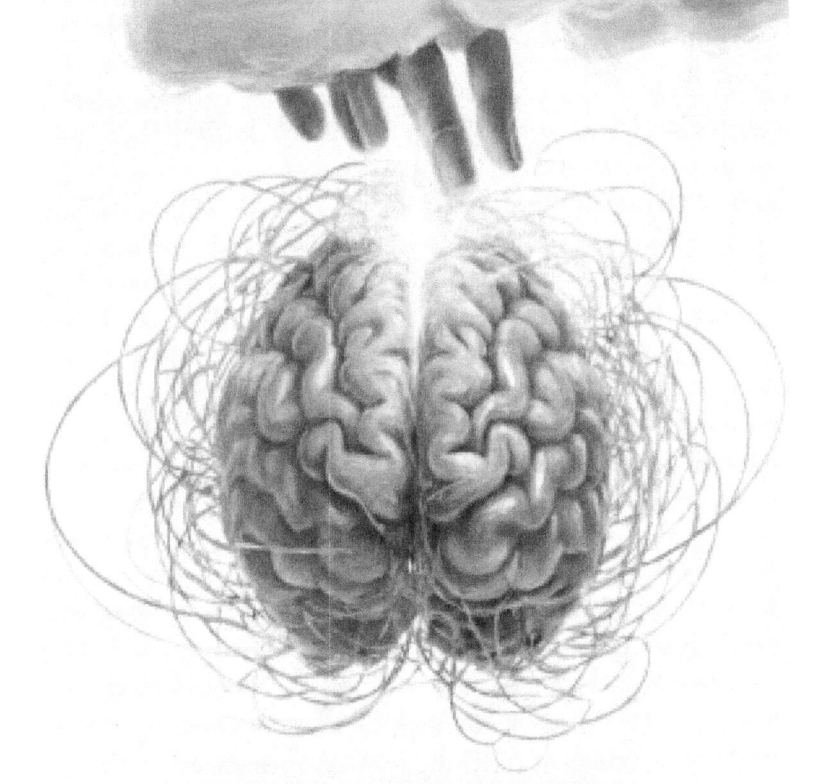

ON THE OTHER SIDE OF FEAR IS YOUR FREEDOM

Trina Raeford

Trina Raeford

Overcoming Anxiety GOD's Way © 2025 Mattrina Raeford.
All rights reserved.

No part of this publication may be reproduced, stored in a retrieval system, or transmitted in any form or by any means — electronic, mechanical, photocopying, recording, or otherwise — without the prior written permission of the author, except in the case of brief quotations used in reviews or articles.

Scripture quotations are taken from the following versions of the Holy Bible:

Holy Bible, King James Version. (1769/2017). Cambridge University Press.

Holy Bible, New International Version. (2011). Zondervan.

Holy Bible, New King James Version. (1982). Thomas Nelson.

Used by permission. All rights reserved.

To book Trina Raeford for a speaking engagement, visit www.anxietydefeated.com

For more information about this book, send email to trina@anxietydefeated.com

Library of Congress Cataloging-in-Publication Data
has been applied for.

ISBN: 979-8-218-85650-2
Printed in the United States of America
First Edition

Dedications

To GOD, who taught me to braid my pain into purpose and light.

To my husband Jon, Thank you for your love, your steady hands in the dark, and your faith in me. I am grateful for this lifelong journey with you — there is so much more to come.

To my children, your dreams moved me, your laughter lifted me, and your future made me fearless. Thank you for being my motivation.

To Mommy, whose love let me wander, discover, and become — thank you for giving me permission to be me.

To Apostle Alfred and Diana Reeves, with deep gratitude for the spiritual foundation of God's Word you laid in my life. Without it, I would have been lost.

For my sister, I write it for the life you deserved and the lives you still change.

For anyone who has felt small or ashamed because of anxiety: this book is with you and for you.

CONTENTS

Dedications	03
How I Got Here	05
How it Started	09
The Truth Shall Make You Free	16
The Break-In	23
The Freedom Plan	40
GOD + Therapy	79
Fearless and Afraid	92
This Means War	99
Overcomer	108
Stay Connected	116
References	117

CHAPTER

Introduction

How I Got Here

I will never forget the first time that he showed up. Stricken with grief and worn down from a long weekend, I was completely defenseless against him. After I took off my clothes and climbed into bed, my heart started to race. I began thinking that it was finally going to happen this time. I had cheated death for as long as I could, my payment had finally come due, and much like my sister this was it for me. But something deep inside me rebelled. It wasn't over—not yet. I wasn't half the woman my sister was, and I knew I needed more time to even get close. My heart was pounding so hard I could feel it in my throat. I leaped out of bed, trembling, and threw my clothes back on. Startled by the commotion, my husband was yanked from his dreamland into my nightmare. I told him I was having a heart attack, and we needed to get to the hospital. Half-dressed and panicked, we bolted down the stairs and into the car. The hospital was thirty minutes away—thirty agonizing minutes between life and death, or so I believed. Every second felt like a roller coaster plunging deeper into fear. I screamed at my husband to drive faster, to ignore the traffic lights. He looked terrified, but he kept his composure long enough to tell me to calm down and pray. But I was far too afraid for prayer. I could barely form a thought beyond Please, God, just let me live. When we finally arrived at the hospital, the first thing that greeted us was the dreaded paperwork. I swear, you could be DOA, and they'd still ask you to fill out that awful paperwork. With the desecrated trees laid across my lap and trembling hands, I managed to remember my date of-birth, social security number, and insurer. To their credit, the staff did act quickly once they saw my condition. I was rushed to the back, vitals taken, and monitored. Hours passed as I lay there shivering beneath a sheet that felt like one-ply toilet paper. My husband begged for a blanket, and when one finally came, I drifted off to sleep. It was 1am when I finally escaped into the dreamland that I had stolen from him earlier. Just as I leaped over the fluffy white clouds, I was jolted from my place of solace by the doctor who finally decided to show up to this fiasco. He informed me I hadn't had a heart attack. Something else had happened. Something more sinister. I had suffered a panic attack. Shame washed over me like cold water. All that chaos—for nothing. I felt like a paranoid fool. Who thinks they're dying when they're not? I was certain the next stop was a mental hospital. I stayed silent on the ride home, too tired and too humiliated to speak. But beneath that silence was determination. Someone had lied to me—some voice inside had convinced me I was dying—and I needed to find out why. When I got home, I sat in the dark and began searching online, scrolling through article after article. Eventually, I reached a simple conclusion: I was afraid to die. My father died at sixty-eight from prostate cancer. He hadn't seen a doctor since 1975, and by the time he did, the cancer had spread to his bones. After the treatments began affecting his vision, he decided he was done fighting and would accept what time he had left. They gave him six months; he lived another eighteen. His illness brought my sister and I closer than ever, but our reunion was short-lived. She died just three months after he did—from an enlarged heart. She'd struggled with high blood pressure for years but never could get it under control. She was the kindest person I've ever known—she truly had a big heart in every sense. After losing them both, was it really so unreasonable to be afraid to die? I justified my fear. I took comfort in it. And slowly, it took over my life. The panic attacks came more

---

On the Other Side of Fear is Your Freedom

frequently, triggered by the smallest things. Once, I was sitting in a friend's chilly living room when it hit me. I tried to sit still and act normal, but inside I was crumbling. When I finally told them what was happening, they barely reacted—as if I'd said I was taking a walk. They couldn't understand that I was fighting for my sanity. Another time, I had a panic attack during a war movie. I'd never been to war, but that one scene sent me spiraling. Soon, I was scared of everything. The attacks came without warning, and after months of being told that I was dying every day, I knew I needed help. I booked a virtual appointment with a counselor at the VA hospital. Working with her felt like an answered prayer. She taught me how to disengage from my fight-or-flight mode and introduced me to techniques for managing anxiety. Before long, I recognized my triggers, anticipated attacks, and used my coping tools with ease. Life began to feel manageable again. But then, my mind adapted. It outsmarted the tricks. I had to invent new ones, and when those failed, the panic attacks returned—less frequent, but enough to remind me I wasn't free. I didn't want to just manage anxiety anymore. I wanted victory. I didn't want control—I wanted deliverance. I wanted to overcome anxiety God's way.

On the Other Side of Fear is Your Freedom

FEAR

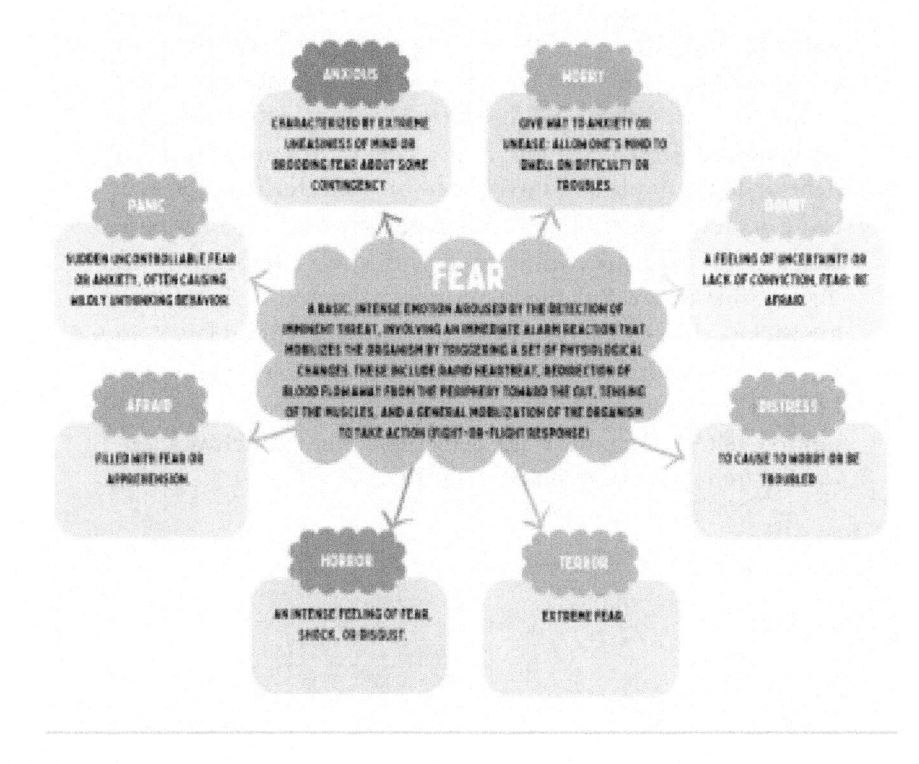

A basic, intense emotion aroused by the detection of imminent threat, involving an immediate alarm reaction that mobilizes the organism by triggering a set of physiological changes. These include rapid heartbeat, redirection of blood flow away from the periphery toward the gut, tensing of the muscles, and a general mobilization of the organism to take action (fight-or-flight response).

ANXIOUS — Characterized by extreme uneasiness of mind or brooding fear about some contingency.

WORRY — Give way to anxiety or unease; allow one's mind to dwell on difficulty or troubles.

PANIC — Sudden uncontrollable fear or anxiety, often causing wildly unthinking behavior.

DOUBT — A feeling of uncertainty or lack of conviction, fear; be afraid.

AFRAID — Filled with fear or apprehension.

DISTRESS — To cause to worry or be troubled.

HORROR — An intense feeling of fear, shock, or disgust.

TERROR — Extreme fear.

CHAPTER
One

How It Started

He goes by many names, but we have come to know him as Fear. If you are going to destroy something, then it is often a good idea to understand where it came from in the first place. In the book of Genesis, we are granted this picturesque account of creation, with Adam and Eve planted in the midst of paradise. But with one act of disobedience, sin entered the world—and brought his companion, fear, alongside him. Genesis 3:10 says, "And he said, I heard thy voice in the garden, and I was afraid, because I was naked; and I hid myself"*(Holy Bible, KJV, 2017)*. As a result, our world is now covered in sin and draped with fear, and our only means of escape is through our Lord and Savior, Jesus Christ. We are gripped by fear at birth—when we exit our maternal comfort and enter into a world of chaos. From that moment, fear gains access to our lives, lurking around every corner, waiting for an opportunity to manifest itself in the craftsmanship of God. And just like any other seed that we plant, it must be watered in order to grow. While we are children, Fear hides and disguises itself in the form of pleasure. Innocent games such as peek-a-boo or being tossed into the air begin our plight of comfort with Fear. Instead of seeing him for the horror that he is, we welcome him as a fun friend. During adolescence, we indulge in the pleasure of fear at amusement parks and while watching scary movies, unknowingly deepening our comfort and desensitization to it. And when we are adults, fear finally emerges as the monster that he truly is—and without Jesus Christ, we are completely defenseless. Science teaches us that fear is a vital survival mechanism—a critical part of human evolution that has protected our species for millions of years. Yet in 2 Timothy 1:7, the Bible says, "For God hath not given us the spirit of fear; but of power, and of love, and of a sound mind" (KJV, 2Timothy 1:7). This seeming contradiction between science and scripture challenges us to look deeper. If fear is so natural, why would God reject it as something He did not give us? The key lies in the distinction between fear as a physical reaction and fear as a spiritual presence. One is biological—triggered by a threat to our safety or well-being. The other is spiritual—an oppressive force that seeks to disconnect us from trust, faith, peace, and God's presence. The spirit of fear is not merely an emotion; it's an entity—a presence. It speaks, it manipulates, it distorts. It tells us we are not safe, even when we are. It convinces us that God won't come through. It blinds us to love and clouds the mind so we can't think clearly. The spirit of fear is not a survival tool—it's a spiritual thief.

> "For God hath not given us the spirit of fear; but of power, and of love, and of a sound mind"
> (KJV, 2Timothy 1:7).

And that's why Paul makes the distinction: God has not given us that spirit. Instead, God gives us a different set of tools:

- **Power** – the ability to act, to rise above, to stand firm in the face of darkness.
- **Love** – a force that casts out fear, bringing connection, compassion, and courage (KJV, 1John 4:18).
- **Sound Mind** – clarity, wisdom, discernment, and peace that transcends panic.

These gifts are not rooted in reaction but in relationship—with God, with truth, and with our divine identity. So while fear may

---

On the Other Side of Fear is Your Freedom

have helped our ancestors run from lions, the spirit of fear is what now keeps us running from God's promises. It is the spiritual voice that says, *"You're not good enough," "You'll fail," "What if?"*—a thousand subtle lies that distract us from walking in faith. As we write this chapter in our lives, we must begin to see fear not as a signal to submit, but as a signal to stand. Not as a guide, but as a gatekeeper. Fear often guards the very places where our freedom and purpose await. And while our bodies may tremble, our spirits do not have to. To live free from the spirit of fear is not to live without challenge—but to live anchored in truth. Fear will knock, but it doesn't have to be invited in. When we realize that fear is not from God, we stop giving it authority. We learn to speak back—with power, with love, and with a sound mind.

Fear is the root. Anxiety is the fruit.
Fear is a spirit that enters through the doorway of uncertainty, trauma, or perceived danger. It begins as a whisper—subtle, deceptive, and invasive. But when it is left unchecked, unchallenged, or misunderstood, fear takes root in the soul. Over time, this root doesn't just stay buried; it produces something—anxiety. Anxiety is the offspring of fear. It is fear matured, internalized, and multiplied. Fear gives birth to anxiety when we don't confront it—when we feed it with what ifs—when we replay the same scenarios in our mind over and over again. But anxiety isn't part of our spiritual design. It is not a divine inheritance. It is the byproduct of entertaining fear too long. Instead of recognizing fear as a spiritual intruder, we begin to adapt to it—build our decisions around it, shape our identity by it, and even normalize its presence. We stop calling it fear and start calling it *personality* or *just how I am*. Think of fear as a seed sown by the enemy—small, but full of potential. When nurtured with doubt, isolation, and silence, it grows into anxiety—a constant hum of dread that plays in the background of our daily lives. It affects our breathing, our sleeping, our relationships, and our ability to hear God's voice clearly. Where fear is sharp and loud—an alarm—anxiety is subtle and persistent—like static. It doesn't always scream. Sometimes it whispers, *"You're not safe," "You're*

On the Other Side of Fear is Your Freedom

not enough," or *"It's all going to fall apart."* It wears the face of concern, caution, or even logic. But its root is always fear. And the deeper that fear grows, the more anxiety becomes a lens through which we view life, rather than a condition we can overcome. When you recognize that fear is not from God, you can also recognize that anxiety is not your portion. Anxiety is not your identity; it's a signal. Somewhere, fear has been planted—and it's time to dig it up. To heal from anxiety, we must go to the root. We must expose fear for what it is: a liar, a thief, and a counterfeit spirit. And we must return to what God has given us—power, love, and a sound mind. Anxiety loses its power when we confront the fear that birthed it. The fact of the matter is, we never needed fear to survive—it needed us. The good news is that God is not afraid of your fear. He meets you in it, invites you to confront it, and walks with you through it—because on the other side of your fear is your freedom. The American Psychological Association defines anxiety as "an emotion characterized by apprehension and somatic symptoms of tension in which an individual anticipates impending danger, catastrophe, or misfortune. The body often mobilizes itself to meet the perceived threat: muscles become tense, breathing quickens, and the heart beats more rapidly. Anxiety may be distinguished from fear both conceptually and physiologically, although the two terms are often used interchangeably. Anxiety is considered a future-oriented, long-acting response broadly focused on a diffuse threat, whereas fear is an appropriate, present-oriented, and short-lived response to a clearly identifiable and specific threat" (American Psychological Association, n.d.).

> **Biological Fear** the body's correct response to a real, present, identifiable threat (like a snake in front of you).

> **Anxiety** the body's fear response misfiring, activating as if there were danger, even when no real or immediate threat exists. Biological fear reacts to what is, anxiety reacts to what might be.

The spirit of fear is not just an emotion; it is an oppressive force, a demonic entity designed to dominate and hinder faith.

On the Other Side of Fear is Your Freedom

It opposes the Spirit of God, who gives believers power, love, and a sound mind *(KJV, 2Timothy 1:7)*. The spirit of fear seeks to replace trust in God with dread, uncertainty, and torment.

Manifestations of the Spirit of Fear

1. Emotional and Physical Signs

a. Anxiety and panic (the *"offspring"* of fear)
b. Heart palpitations and restlessness.
c. Constant sense of dread or doom.

2. Mental and Spiritual Effects

a. **Discouragement:** Whispering lies that convince someone they will fail if they step out in faith.
b. **Paralysis:** Preventing forward movement by magnifying past failures and future uncertainties.
c. **False Accusations:** Stirring up self-condemnation and doubt about salvation or worthiness.
d. **Hopelessness:** Stealing vision and confidence in God's promises.

Strategies of the Spirit of Fear

- Keeps people focused on the *"what ifs"* instead of God's faithfulness.
- Replays past mistakes to create shame and stagnation.
- Magnifies risks while minimizing God's ability to sustain.
- Sows lies of condemnation to distance believers from God.

Fear is the root of anxiety, and anxiety is deeply complex because it touches every part of a person's being. Anxiety doesn't remain in the mind alone; it filters into the body, soul, spirit, will, and emotions, creating a ripple effect that impacts how a person

---

On the Other Side of Fear is Your Freedom

thinks, feels, and lives. In the mind, it can manifest as racing thoughts, constant worry, or intrusive fears. In the body, it often shows up through tension, restlessness, fatigue, or physical symptoms like headaches, stomach problems, and even heart palpitations. In the soul, it can bring weariness, discouragement, and a sense of hopelessness. In the spirit, it tries to weaken faith, cloud discernment, and create distance from God through doubt and fear of the future. It also affects the will, making it harder for someone to make decisions or move forward, and it entangles the emotions, often producing feelings of dread, sadness, or instability. This all-encompassing influence is why anxiety feels so heavy and hard to overcome—it doesn't just attack one area, but seeks to overwhelm the entire person. This is a big part of why anxiety is often difficult to treat. Because anxiety doesn't affect just one part of a person, but the whole person, it requires a holistic approach to healing. If someone only addresses anxiety at the mental level (thoughts and worries), but not the body, spirit, emotions, or will, then the root influence remains, and the person often feels like they are only putting a *"band-aid"* over a deeper wound.

Here's why this makes treatment complex:

1. Multiple Layers of Impact

- **Mind**: Anxious thought patterns can be deeply ingrained and need intentional renewal.
- **Body**: Physical symptoms like restlessness, fatigue, or palpitations create a cycle where the body reinforces the anxiety in the mind.
- **Soul/Emotions**: When discouragement or hopelessness sets in, it can feel overwhelming, fueling more fear.
- **Spirit**: If faith is weakened and fear dominates, anxiety is spiritually magnified.
- **Will**: Difficulty making decisions or moving forward keeps a person *"stuck,"* reinforcing the sense of paralysis.

On the Other Side of Fear is Your Freedom

2. Spirit vs. Natural

Anxiety is often treated only as a medical or psychological issue, but it also has a spiritual dimension. Fear, as a spirit, seeks to oppress faith. If the spiritual root is not addressed, treatment may feel incomplete, even if therapy or medication helps the symptoms.

3. The Cycle of Reinforcement

Each area feeds into the other. For example: anxious thoughts **(mind)** cause rapid heartbeat **(body)**, which makes the person more fearful **(emotions)**, which weakens faith **(spirit)**, and eventually discourages action **(will)**. Breaking this cycle takes intentional work.

Though anxiety is complex, healing is possible. The same way anxiety touches the whole person, God's power can reach and heal every part of us. His Word renews the mind, His Spirit strengthens the inner being, His presence calms the emotions, and His promises restore the will to choose faith over fear. Anxiety may touch the whole person, but so does the healing power of Christ.

On the Other Side of Fear is Your Freedom

CHAPTER Two

The Truth Shall Make You Free

Have you ever had that bad feeling that someone is lying to you? You don't know how or why, but you sense the lie. Things just aren't adding up. You may persistently challenge that person, but to no avail — they are willing to die with the lie. And when the truth stays hidden, it feels like defeat—like somehow the lie has won. Lies create confusion, keep you bound, and leave you questioning not just the situation but sometimes yourself. People often say, *"What I don't know can't hurt me,"* but this couldn't be further from the truth. One of the clearest examples of how not knowing can hurt comes from relationships—especially marriage. Imagine a spouse who is being cheated on but doesn't know it. They sense something is wrong — the distance, the excuses, the late nights — but without the truth, they blame themselves. They wonder if they're not attractive enough, not fun enough, not good enough. That hidden betrayal eats away at their confidence, their trust, and even their sense of worth. They suffer in silence because they don't know the reality of what's happening. But when the truth finally comes out — as painful as it is in the beginning — it brings clarity. The lies stop. The confusion and self-blame begin to lift. Instead of asking, *"What's wrong with me?"* they can see the real problem wasn't their fault. The truth might break their heart, but it also breaks the chains of deception that were slowly destroying them. Knowing the truth gives them the chance to heal, to rebuild their life, and to move forward in freedom. Sometimes the truth saves a marriage through repentance and restoration; other times, it gives the innocent partner the strength to walk away. Either way, the truth, though painful, is what allows healing to finally begin. Anxiety is no different. It operates in deception, feeding on lies and half-truths, and it doesn't want you to understand the spiritual component attached to it. That's why it doesn't resist when people turn only to counseling or medication — because while those things can provide help and relief, if the truth of God's Word is never applied, anxiety knows it can still keep its grip. Scripture warns us, "My people perish for lack of knowledge" (*Holy Bible, KJV, Hosea* 4:6). What we don't know can destroy us. But Jesus also promised, "You shall know the truth, and the truth shall make you free." That truth is not just information; it is revelation. It is the living Word of God shining into the lies that keep us bound, breaking the cycle of fear and oppression, and bringing the freedom that nothing else can give. Then said Jesus to those Jews which believed on him, "if ye continue in my word, then are ye my disciples indeed; and ye shall know the truth, and the truth shall make you free" (*KJV, John* 8:31-32). You often hear people say, "the truth shall set you free." At first glance, setting someone free and making someone free might seem like the same thing. But spiritually—and even practically—they carry very different meanings. To be set free means to be released from something that once held you captive. It's an act of liberation, but it doesn't guarantee lasting freedom. Chains may be broken, but the root—the yoke—can still remain. It's freedom from the outside in. To be made free, however, is something far deeper. It speaks to transformation. It's not just a release—it's a re-creation. You're not just removed from captivity—you're redefined. Made new. Renewed in mindset, in identity, and in truth. It's freedom from the inside out. This is why someone can be set free from anxiety through counseling, medication, or self-help—and it works for a time. But often, that spirit returns. The fear creeps back in. The anxiety resurfaces.

On the Other Side of Fear is Your Freedom

And the cycle repeats. Why? Because being set free addresses the symptoms. But being made free addresses the source. And Jesus didn't come just to set you free. He came to make you free. "If the Son therefore shall make you free, ye shall be free indeed" (KJV, John 8:36). Made free by truth. Made free by Him. Made free in a way that breaks chains and destroys yokes. Until you are made free by truth—by Christ Himself—freedom will always be temporary. But when you are made free, the cycle is broken, not managed. The spirit of anxiety has nowhere to return to—because your house has been made new. True freedom lies in truth. Freedom cannot operate through lies—it cannot breathe in deception. Where there is falsehood, fear thrives. Where there is confusion, anxiety grows. But where truth is present, chains break. This is why, to be free from anxiety—not just momentarily relieved, but truly and spiritually free—you must know the truth. Not a temporary fact. Not a motivational quote. Not a fleeting feeling. But the Truth. And the only truth I know, the only one that has ever made me free, is Jesus Christ. He does not just speak truth—He is Truth. John 14:6 says, "I am the way, the truth, and the life..."(KJV, John 14:6). He is not an option; He is the origin. He is not an escape; He is the answer. He doesn't manage fear—He casts it out. When Jesus enters, lies lose their power. When Jesus speaks, anxiety has to silence itself. When Jesus reigns, fear must bow. So if you want freedom from anxiety, you need more than coping tools—you need truth. You need Him. Freedom isn't found in ignoring fear. It's not found in pretending anxiety isn't real. Freedom is found when you replace the lie—*"I am not safe, I am not loved, I am not enough"*—with the Truth: *"I am His. I am seen. I am safe. I am loved."* Jesus is the Truth that disarms fear. He is the light that exposes the spirit of anxiety. And when He speaks over your life, He doesn't say, *"Try harder."* He says,"Peace, be still"(KJV, Mark 4:39). That is the Truth. And the Truth is what makes you free. I pray that if you made it to this point in the book you are delivered. For some, freedom will come in an instant—according to your faith, it will break like a flood. But if you're anything like me, it may not happen all at once. It will take time. It took time for the lie to take

---

On the Other Side of Fear is Your Freedom

root in your heart—layer by layer, word by word, experience by experience. And in the same way, it may take time for the truth to settle in and undo what fear has built. Don't be discouraged by the process. The lie was planted gradually, and now the truth is being planted too—one truth at a time, one moment at a time. And every time you choose truth over fear, you are reclaiming ground. You are being made free. Anxiety is going to tell you that you're not free. That this book is nonsense. That a few words could never undo the damage he's done. And he won't just say it with words—he'll try to prove it by making you feel the weight of his plunder. The tension in your chest. The racing thoughts. The dread that creeps in uninvited. But hear me clearly: I never said that accepting the truth means you won't feel anything. I never promised you wouldn't go through anything. What I am saying is this—he wants you to give up. He wants you to doubt the truth. And in the coming days, he's going to throw everything he has at you. But it won't be enough. Because what our Lord and Savior, Jesus Christ, has equipped you with is greater. Stronger. Eternal. Anxiety may scream, but the truth will stand. Fear may perform, but the cross already won. So when it gets heavy—when the feelings come, when the lies get loud—remember this: Don't trust the show. Trust the truth. Hold on. Believe. And no matter what you feel, no matter what you face—remember what's real. And the only thing that's real, the only thing that never changes, is the truth. And the truth is Jesus. When we understand that fear and anxiety are spiritual forces, we also begin to understand why their effects show up in our physical bodies. Racing hearts. Shaky hands. Tight chests. Sleepless nights. It's not your imagination—your body feels what your spirit is fighting. But just because your body is reacting doesn't mean your spirit has to agree. Your body is responding to old patterns, to past trauma, to practiced worry, to spiritual noise. But your body is not in charge—your spirit is. So what do you say when your body is overwhelmed, even though you know fear is not from God? You speak truth out loud. You bring your spirit into alignment with God's Word and then command your body to come into agreement too. Try saying things like: *I feel*

On the Other Side of Fear is Your Freedom

fear, but I am not ruled by fear. Body, you are safe. Mind, you are sound. Heart, you are guarded by peace. This tension is not truth. God's presence is my reality. I am not in danger. I am not alone. God is with me, and He is not afraid. Even though I walk through the valley, I will not fear. He is with me." You don't deny what your body feels—you acknowledge it, but you don't give it the final word. Your body might be conditioned to expect chaos, but you are re-teaching it peace. This takes practice. And grace. And time. Sometimes you'll feel the fear and still choose peace. Other times, you'll feel like peace is far away—but you'll still speak it until your body begins to respond. Remember: healing is not pretending you don't feel fear. Healing is learning to walk in truth even when fear is present, until fear no longer controls the conversation. And the more you walk in truth, the more your body will learn to follow your spirit—not the spirit of fear. This isn't going to be a one-time battle. It's a daily fight—a war waged in the quiet moments, when you're tired, when your spirit is low, when the day has been hard and your guard is down. Anxiety waits for those moments. But we are not defenseless. We fight anxiety with truth. Not just any truth—but the living, breathing Word of God. We've already learned one powerful affirmation: "God has not given us the spirit of fear; but of power, and of love, and of a sound mind" *(KJV, 2 Timothy 1:7)*. That verse alone is enough to stop fear in its tracks—but God didn't stop there. He gave us more. Another powerful weapon is found in Philippians 4:6-7: "Be anxious for nothing, but in everything by prayer and supplication, with thanksgiving, let your requests be made known to God; and the peace of God, which surpasses all understanding, will guard your hearts and minds through Christ Jesus" *(KJV, Philippians 4:6-7)*. Notice—His peace doesn't just calm you, it guards you. That means anxiety has to get through Him before it can get to you. And God even tells us how to train our minds so fear has no place to land. Philippians 4:8 says: "Finally, brethren, whatever things are true, whatever things are noble, whatever things are just, whatever things are pure, whatever things are lovely, whatever things are of good report—if there is any virtue and if there is anything praisewor-

---

On the Other Side of Fear is Your Freedom

thy—meditate on these things"*(KJV, Philippians 4:8)*. Your thoughts shape your atmosphere. And God has given us the blueprint for peace—not just in theory, but in practice. Philippians 4:9 continues: "The things which you learned and received and heard and saw in me—these do, and the God of peace will be with you"*(KJV, Philippians 4:9)*. This is not passive. This is spiritual warfare. This is how we fight back: With truth. With prayer. With gratitude. With obedience. And most of all—with God's presence, walking beside us every step of the way.

The Invitation to Freedom

I have to be honest with you—this book will only truly work for believers. At first, I tried to write this objectively, hoping it could reach everyone, no matter where they stood in their faith. But the deeper I went, the clearer it became: truth isn't a concept—it's a person. And that person is Jesus Christ. You cannot have lasting freedom from anxiety without first receiving the One who is Truth itself. Only when Jesus becomes your Lord and Savior do you receive the authority, the identity, and the spiritual power to stand against anxiety and every other enemy of your soul. Without Him, you may find temporary relief—but never full deliverance. With Him, you don't just manage anxiety—you overcome it. God's way is the only way.

If you're ready to take that step, I invite you to read Romans 10:9-10, 13 *(Holy Bible, NKJV, 1982)*. It says: "That if you confess with your mouth the Lord Jesus and believe in your heart that GOD has raised Him from the dead, you will be saved. For with the heart one believes unto righteousness, and with the mouth confession is made unto salvation. For whoever calls on the name of the Lord shall be saved" *(NKJV, Romans 10:9-10, 13)*. If you believe these words, I encourage you—right here, right now—to talk to Jesus. Tell Him you believe. Tell Him you receive Him into your heart and your life. Tell Him you want to be made new and walk in His truth. I know this may sound like religious talk—maybe even propaganda. But let's be real:

On the Other Side of Fear is Your Freedom

you've tried everything else. And if you're still reading, it's because deep down, you know something's still missing. This is the only way to eradicate anxiety at the root. You must surrender to the One who made you. You must do it God's way.

On the Other Side of Fear is Your Freedom

CHAPTER
Three

The Break-In

You pull into your driveway at the end of a long day, ready to sink into the comfort of your home. But something feels off. The front door is cracked open, just enough for your stomach to knot. Your first thought is, did I forget to lock it? But when you step closer, you see the splintered wood around the doorframe. The lock has been broken. Heart pounding, you push the door open. Instantly, your worst fears are confirmed. The house looks like a storm tore through it. Drawers have been yanked open and dumped onto the floor. Cabinets hang open like wounded mouths. Belongings you once treasured are scattered, broken, or missing. You walk further in, stunned. The living room no longer feels like your safe space; it feels violated. The couch cushions have been slashed open. Family photos have been pulled from their frames. Your favorite blanket — the one you wrapped yourself in on hard nights — is gone. The deeper you go, the more you realize the thief didn't just want things; he wanted pieces of you. In the bedroom, your jewelry box sits empty. Your favorite outfit is missing, the one you wore when you felt most confident. Even the small, seemingly worthless trinkets that carried priceless memories have been stolen. This wasn't just theft — this was an invasion. It was personal. But then comes the most chilling discovery. As you look around, it dawns on you: the thief hasn't just taken your possessions. He's taken something more precious. He's stolen your joy. Your peace. Your confidence. Even your voice. The very things that made this house a home — and made you you — are gone. You stand in the middle of the wreckage, stunned, realizing the house doesn't just feel empty. You feel empty. And then it hits you: the thief's name is Anxiety. He doesn't break into homes — he breaks into hearts and minds. He doesn't just strip away what you have — he strips away who you are. He disguises himself in your skin, wearing you like a suit until even your closest friends no longer recognize you. They see your fear, silence and experience your trauma. At first, you didn't even notice him slip in. He started small. A restless night here. A worry there. A sense of unease that you dismissed as *"just stress."* But little by little, the thief became bolder. He took your laughter and replaced it with doubt. He stole your ability to dream and left you with *"what ifs."* He swapped out your boldness for hesitation. And without realizing it, you started to shrink. This is the crime of anxiety: it convinces you to hand over your identity piece by piece, until you can no longer remember who you were before he showed up. It whispers the lie that your struggles define you, that your wounds are your worth, that your fear is your future. But let me tell you the truth. Anxiety may be a thief, but he is not your master. He may have broken in, but he does not own the house. He may be loud, but he does not get the final word. It may wear your face for a season, but it cannot erase your name. Your identity was written by God long before anxiety ever crept through the door, and no thief — not even this one — has the power to erase what GOD Himself has sealed. Spiritually, anxiety shows no signs of forced entry, and you're left wondering how it slipped past your defenses. Who gave anxiety access to you? Who opened the door and let him in? The answer is simple: you did. Anxiety didn't break in—it was invited. Not all at once, but little by little. Each time you entertained a lie, each time you replayed a fear, each time you let worry linger instead of shutting it down at the door, you cracked it open wider. Until one day, anxiety walked right in and made himself at home. Unchecked behavior means you

---

On the Other Side of Fear is Your Freedom

agree. Every time you allow anxiety to linger unchallenged, you silently nod in agreement with its lies. You may not say it out loud, but your inaction is consent. When fear speaks and you don't confront it with truth, you're giving it permission to keep talking. When worry repeats the same scenario over and over and you don't shut it down, you're agreeing to its version of reality. The enemy counts on your silence. He counts on you being too tired, too distracted, or too unsure to confront him. Because the longer you leave that behavior unchecked, the stronger his foothold becomes. But the moment you expose it, name it, and refuse to agree with it, you strip it of power. Anxiety cannot break in by force. He has no power unless it's given to him. And here's the worst part: he knows this. Do you? You are the owner of the house. You have the keys. You have the authority to determine who stays and who goes. Yet for too long, you've allowed the intruder to set up camp, sit on your couch, and act like he belongs there. It's time to get him out of your house. Stop introducing him to people as if he's part of the family. He is not your companion. He is not your comfort. He is your enemy — in complete opposition of everything God placed inside of you. While you've been smiling on the outside, he's been stealing your stuff on the inside. He whispers lies in your ear even when you know the truth. And you know he's lying — yet you still believe him. How do we know you believe him? Because your body tells on you. Your sleepless nights, your shallow breathing, your racing thoughts, your shrinking confidence — they're all evidence of belief in the intruder's lies. Before you know it, you've welcomed anxiety into your daily routine without even realizing it. That's the danger: it convinces you it belongs, that it's just a part of who you are, when in reality it's an intruder robbing you of everything he can get his hands on. If you believe the thief's lies, you hand him the keys to the house. But if you believe God's truth, you slam the door in his face. You determine what gets to live in your house and it starts with what you believe. Many of us have tried to help out a friend who was only supposed to stay for a night, and before you know it, they've set up camp. Or maybe you've dealt with the

---

On the Other Side of Fear is Your Freedom

uninvited guest who somehow begins living in your house, and you're too nice to tell them this was never the plan. Even if you haven't experienced this personally, you've probably heard the horror stories of what happens when you try to kick them out. Suddenly they have rights, and you can't just put them on the streets. God forbid they've been given a key! My friend, you have an uninvited guest called Anxiety. Whether you accidentally allowed him in or trauma opened the door, he is not leaving without a fight. Why would he just walk away? He's comfortable now. He's been living rent-free in your mind, eating on your dime, and draining your spirit. Anxiety is that *"friend"* you tried to help out, but instead of showing gratitude, he took advantage of your kindness and turned your life upside down. Living with anxiety has cost you more than you realize. And if you're not a fighter, you may just keep hoping one day life will go back to normal—that if you're nice enough, maybe he'll pack up and leave on his own. But hear me: he won't. He has no intention of leaving unless you stand up and make him go. It's not the kind of fight you may be imagining. At times it will feel like you're fighting yourself, and that's exactly what he wants you to believe. But the fight isn't against you—it's against him. And the only way to win is to stand on God's Word. Not just hold onto it quietly, but speak it out loud. Speak it back to anxiety every time he opens his ugly mouth. You've seen a "yuck mouth" before—the kind that makes you cringe. That's the mouth anxiety has been running inside your clean body. It's time to shut it permanently with the truth of God's Word. After a break-in, the first thing you to do is take inventory of what's missing. You walk through each room, write down what was taken, and begin to see the scope of the loss. Spiritually the same process is necessary. When is the last time you sat down and took inventory of what's missing in your life? Go back to the time before the trauma, before anxiety showed up at your door. What did you have then that you don't have now? What was taken? Was it joy, peace, or your confidence that has been stolen? Until you identify what's gone, you won't know what you need to reclaim. That's why the inventory matters—it's not just about recognizing the loss, it's about mapping the path

---

On the Other Side of Fear is Your Freedom

to restoration. The next step after any break-in is getting protection. No one leaves their door unlocked after a thief has walked through it once. You install stronger locks, add an alarm, maybe even cameras. You do what it takes so you won't be caught off guard again. Spiritually, the same is true. How will you guard your heart and mind so that Anxiety doesn't keep slipping back in unnoticed? What armor, habits, or boundaries can you put in place so that if he dares to come knocking again, you are ready— not cowering, but prepared to stand your ground? Once he realizes that he is caught, get ready for the manipulation and lies to come full force. The enemy does not release his grip easily. He wants to ensure his foothold remains, so he will throw everything he has at you. And the first area he will attack is your emotions. Why? Because experience has taught him that this is where he has always been able to get you. He knows the triggers, the patterns, and the weaknesses that have worked before. The enemy studies you. He knows the moments when you're tired, overwhelmed, or stretched thin. He knows which words sting, which memories haunt, and which fears make your chest tighten. And because emotions are powerful— God-designed signals that tell us something is happening inside of us—the enemy twists them and uses them against us. What was meant to help you process becomes a weapon to paralyze you. Think about it: how many times have you said, *"I just don't feel like God is near"* or, *"I feel like things will never change."* Those statements aren't truth—they're feelings. But if you let those feelings take the driver's seat, they shape your decisions, your perspective, and your faith. That's exactly what the enemy wants. He doesn't have to steal your salvation; he just has to convince you to interpret God's truth through the lens of your emotions instead of interpreting your emotions through the lens of God's truth. This is emotional warfare. And it's subtle. He doesn't come at you with horns and fire—he comes at you with a wave of fear, a rush of discouragement, a whisper of doubt. His goal is to make you feel defeated long before you actually are. But here's the realization: emotions are real, but they are not rulers. They can inform you, but they should never control you. When you live led

---

On the Other Side of Fear is Your Freedom

by the Spirit, not by your feelings, the enemy loses his greatest weapon. I know you've read a lot. Let's just say you agree with everything up to this point, but now you're left wondering: *How do I actually start? Where do I begin?* You don't rebuild everything overnight. You start the same way you'd begin cleaning up after a break-in—one room at a time, one step at a time. It's easy to get overwhelmed when you think about the whole house, but you can handle one space. Spiritually, the same principle applies.

1. **Start with inventory.** Sit down with God and ask Him to show you what has been stolen—your joy, your peace, your confidence. Write it down. Naming the loss is the first step to reclaiming it.

2. **Seal the cracks.** Reflect on where anxiety has found its entry points. Was it through unchecked thoughts, fear, exhaustion, or isolation? Identifying the access points helps you guard against future intrusions.

3. **Suit up.** Begin putting on the armor of God daily. Even if you don't feel like it, declare His truth over your life. Speak Scripture out loud. Equip yourself piece by piece, knowing that each one strengthens your defense.

4. **Pray with authority.** Break old agreements with anxiety and align yourself with God's Word. Prayer is not just asking—it's declaring, binding, and loosing. It's how you enforce your victory.

Remember: You don't need to have it all figured out before you start. You just need to take one faithful step forward. God meets you in the step.

Before we dive into these steps, I want to address the problem with ownership language and how it defeats you before you ever begin. Too often we speak about anxiety using words that bind us to it: *"my anxiety," "my panic attacks," "my fear."* The moment you call it yours, you give it permission to stay. Ownership language makes the intruder a roommate.

On the Other Side of Fear is Your Freedom

It shifts anxiety from being an unwanted guest to being part of your identity— and that's exactly what the enemy wants. Think about it: would you ever proudly say, *"my cancer"* or *"my thief"*? No, because you don't want ownership of something destructive. Yet with anxiety, we unknowingly put a name tag on it and claim it as our own. That kind of language defeats you before the fight even begins, because how can you resist something you've already accepted as a part of who you are? Anxiety is not who you are, it's what you're experiencing. Your identity is not tied to your struggle; your identity is anchored in Christ. Scripture says, "Therefore, if anyone is in Christ, the new creation has come: The old has gone, the new is here" *(Holy Bible, NIV, 2011, 2Corinthians 5:17)*. That means your words should line up with your new nature, not your old battles. So from this point on, stop calling anxiety *"yours."* It's not yours, it's an intruder. Refuse to give it ownership in your life. The language you use matters, because your words set the tone for your faith. Instead of saying *"my anxiety,"* say: *"The anxiety I experience..." "This intruder..." "The fear that visits..." "The battle I'm facing..."* These shifts remind you that anxiety is something happening to you, not who you are. So, stop letting him stand beside you. Step into the ring. Put on your gloves. Push him to his corner. It's time to put in the work— not to destroy yourself, but to fight the thief who's been masquerading as your friend.

Take Inventory

You may be wondering why this step matters. Why take the time to write things down? Why dig into places you'd rather just move past? The reason is simple: you cannot reclaim what you have not identified. If you don't name it, you'll live without it, assuming the loss is permanent. That's exactly what anxiety wants—to convince you that the things it stole can never be restored.

But when you sit with God and take inventory, you're doing two powerful things:

1. **You're exposing the thief.** A thief doesn't like to be identified. Once you name what's missing, you shine a

---

On the Other Side of Fear is Your Freedom

light on where anxiety has had control, and light always drives darkness away.

2. **You're partnering with God for restoration.** Writing it down is your declaration that these things don't belong to anxiety—they belong to you, and God intends to restore them. Scripture says, "So I will restore to you the years that the swarming locust has eaten..." *(Holy Bible, NKJV, 1982, Joel 2:25).* This is your step of faith to claim what is rightfully yours.

This exercise isn't about reliving the past—it's about reclaiming your future. It's you saying, *"I see what's been taken, and I'm not leaving it in the enemy's hands any longer."*

Reflection Exercise: Taking Inventory
Grab a journal or notebook and take a few quiet moments with God. Ask Him to show you what anxiety has stolen. Don't filter or minimize—be honest. Then, beside each loss, find a Scripture that declares God's promise of restoration.

1. What has anxiety stolen from you?

- My joy → _____
- My peace → _____
- My confidence → _____
- Other (list as needed) → _____

2. What does God's Word say about restoring it?

- **Joy:** "..The joy of the Lord is your strength"*(NKJV, Nehemiah 8:10).*
- **Peace:** "You will keep him in perfect peace, whose mind is stayed on You, because he trust in You"*(NKJV, Isaiah 26:3).*
- **Confidence:** "For the Lord will be your confidence, and will keep your foot from being caught"*(NKJV, Proverbs 3:26).*

On the Other Side of Fear is Your Freedom

Write out at least three personal declarations using your list. For example:

- "My joy belongs to me, and God is restoring it."
- "Peace is mine because Jesus gave it to me."
- "I walk in confidence because the Lord is my strength."

Seal the Cracks

Now that you've taken inventory and identified what's missing, the next question is just as important: How did anxiety get in? After a break-in, you don't just list what was stolen—you check the doors, the windows, the locks. You look for the cracks and weaknesses that gave the thief access. Spiritually, the same process is necessary. If you don't address the entry points, anxiety will find its way back in. That brings us to the next step: sealing the cracks. This is where you begin to fortify your spiritual home so the same intruder can't slip in again. Taking inventory reveals what was lost, but sealing the cracks prevents it from being stolen again. Anxiety doesn't usually break down the front door—it slips in through weaknesses that go unnoticed. Here are some of the most common entry points, and how you can begin to seal them:

- **The crack of unchecked thoughts.**
  One negative thought left unchallenged can spiral into fear. Scripture says, "...We take captive every thought to make it obedient to Christ" *(NIV, 2 Corinthians 10:5)*. Sealing this crack means testing your thoughts: Does this line up with God's Word, or is it a lie?

- **The crack of fear.**
  Fear is often the doorway anxiety walks through. Isaiah 41:10 reminds us, "Fear not, for I am with you; be not dismayed, for I am your God" *(NKJV, Isaiah 41:10)*. Sealing this crack looks like confronting fear with truth—not pretending it's not there, but refusing to let it dictate your steps.

On the Other Side of Fear is Your Freedom

- **The crack of exhaustion.**
  A weary body and mind become easy targets. Even Elijah, a mighty prophet, was overtaken by despair when he was exhausted *(Holy Bible, KJV, 2017, 1Kings 19)*. God's response? Rest, food, and His presence. Sealing this crack means honoring your limits, resting well, and trusting God to sustain you.

- **The crack of isolation.**
  Anxiety grows in silence and secrecy. Ecclesiastes 4:9-10 reminds us that "two are better than one… if either of them falls down, one can help the other up"*(NIV, Ecclesiastes 4:9-10)*. Sealing this crack means staying connected—to God, trusted friends, and/or a faith community.

Sealing the cracks doesn't mean you'll never face another attack. But it does mean that when anxiety comes knocking again, it won't find the same easy way in. Each sealed crack is a declaration that your life is under new management—that the intruder no longer has access to what belongs to God.

Reflection Exercise: Your Spiritual Home Inspection

Before you can seal the cracks, you have to identify them. Take a few quiet moments with God and ask Him to show you where anxiety has found its way in. Use this as your personal "home inspection."

1. Which cracks has anxiety used in your life?

☐ Unchecked thoughts (negative thoughts I allowed to spiral unchecked)

☐ Fear (worry, insecurity, or dread that I let grow)

☐ Exhaustion (running on empty physically, emotionally, or spiritually)

☐ Isolation (pulling away from God or people who could support me)

☐ Other: _____

2. How will I begin to seal this crack?

- With God's Word: _____
- With new habits: _____
- With support/accountability _____

3. My declaration of faith:

Write one sentence declaring that the crack is sealed. Example: *"I take every thought captive to Christ, and I will not let anxiety slip in through lies."*

On the Other Side of Fear is Your Freedom

Suit Up

You've taken inventory of what was stolen. You've sealed the cracks where anxiety slipped in. Now it's time to suit up. Because the truth is, the enemy won't stop trying. He'll circle the block, testing the doors and windows, looking for another way in. That's why God doesn't just tell us to be careful—He tells us to be armed. Paul writes in Ephesians 6:11, "Put on the full armor of God, so that you can take your stand against the devil's schemes"*(NIV, Ephesians 6:11)*. Each piece of armor is a defense against anxiety's lies and attacks, and together they make you unshakable.

The Belt of Truth

Anxiety thrives on lies: *"You're not safe. You're not enough. Things will never change."* The belt of truth holds everything together by reminding you of what God has already said. "And ye shall know the truth, and the truth shall make you free"*(KJV, John 8:32)*. Every time you declare God's Word, you tighten the belt and silence the lies.

The Breastplate of Righteousness

Guilt, shame, and regret are open doors for anxiety. The breastplate guards your heart, reminding you that your righteousness isn't earned—it's given. "This righteousness is given through faith in Jesus Christ to all who believe" *(NIV, Romans 3:22)*. When anxiety says, *"You're not good enough,"* the breastplate answers, *"I am covered by the righteousness of Christ."*

The Shoes of Peace

Anxiety wants you off balance, tripping over fear, running in circles. But God gives you shoes that bring stability. "And the peace of God, which transcends all understanding, will guard your hearts and your minds in Christ Jesus"*(NIV, Philippians 4:7)*. These shoes remind you that peace is not the absence of problems—it's the presence of Christ in the middle of them.

On the Other Side of Fear is Your Freedom

The Shield of Faith
Paul says the shield of faith extinguishes "...all the flaming arrows of the evil one" (NIV, Ephesians 6:16). Those arrows look like racing thoughts, worst-case scenarios, and waves of panic. Faith doesn't ignore them—it blocks them. Faith says, *"My God is bigger than my fears. He is faithful even when I can't see it."*

The Helmet of Salvation
The battlefield of anxiety is almost always in the mind. The helmet of salvation protects your thoughts by reminding you who you belong to and what Christ has done for you. "Take the helmet of salvation...", means covering your mind daily with the truth that you are secure, redeemed, and safe in Him (NIV, Ephesians 6:17).

The Sword of the Spirit
Every other piece of armor is defensive, but the sword is for offense. Paul tells us the sword is the Word of God. Jesus Himself fought off Satan's attacks with Scripture (KJV, Matthew 4:1-11). When anxiety whispers, *"You can't handle this,"* you fight back with "I can do all things through Christ who strengthens me" (KJV, Philippians 4:13). The sword isn't just held—it's spoken.

Suiting up in the armor of God isn't a one-time thing; it's a daily practice. Each morning you choose to put it on, declaring that today you will not fight bare, but fully equipped.

Reflective Exercise: Putting On the Armor
Take a few minutes each morning to *"suit up"* before your day begins. This is not just symbolic—it's a way of aligning your heart, mind, and spirit with God's truth. Use the prompts below as a guide. I encourage you to actually stand up and go through these physically if possible — fastening the belt, pretending to lift a shield, placing the helmet — so your body practices the truth as well as your heart and mind.

On the Other Side of Fear is Your Freedom

Pray With Authority

You've taken inventory of what was stolen. You've sealed the cracks where anxiety used to slip in. You've suited up in the armor of God. Now comes the final step: pray with authority. Prayer is not a whisper of fear; it is a declaration of truth. It's how you enforce heaven's rule on earth. Paul doesn't end his description of the armor of God with the sword—he ends with prayer: "And pray in the Spirit on all occasions with all kinds of prayers and requests..." *(NIV, Ephesians 6:18)*. Prayer is what activates the armor and brings God's power into your situation. When you pray with authority, you are not begging God to do something He has already promised. You are standing on His Word, speaking it out loud, and commanding anxiety to leave because it no longer has the right to stay. Jesus said, "I have given you authority… to overcome all the power of the enemy..." *(NIV, Luke 10:19)*. That authority belongs to you as His child.

Praying with authority means:

- You speak **God's truth** instead of repeating anxiety's lies.
- You **bind and break agreement** with fear in the name of Jesus.
- You **loose peace, joy, and confidence** into your life by declaring God's promises.
- You **remind the enemy** that you are no longer in partnership with him—you belong to Christ.

This is not about volume or emotion—it's about confidence in God's Word. Whether whispered in the quiet of your room or declared boldly in the car on your way to work, prayer with authority is prayer that believes.

End Your Partnership with Anxiety

Heaven won't interfere with what you agree with. Agreement is powerful. Scripture asks, "Can two walk together unless they are agreed?" *(NKJV, Amos 3:3)*. Agreement creates partnership. When you silently agree with the lies of anxiety—whether through unchecked thoughts, repeated behaviors, or unchallenged emotions—you are, in effect, giving anxiety the right to walk alongside you.

- **Agreement looks like:** letting fear sit in your thoughts unchallenged, saying *"this is just who I am,"* or believing *"things will never change."* Every time you let those statements go unchecked, you hand over the key to your peace.

- **Alignment, however, looks different.** Alignment means choosing to line your heart and mind up with God's truth instead of your feelings. It is not denial—it is decision. You are deciding to believe what God says even when your emotions scream the opposite.

When you agree with anxiety, you empower the thief. When you align with God's Word, you invite heaven's authority into your situation. Jesus made this clear: "Truly I tell you, whatever you bind on earth will be bound in heaven, and whatever you loose on earth will be loosed in heaven" *(NIV Matthew 18:18)*. I don't want you to just resist anxiety. I want you to divorce it, break covenant with it, and end your partnership with him forever. Anxiety is not a part of who you are; it's an intruder who has taken advantage of your kindness and stayed far too long. And just like a toxic relationship, the only way to truly heal is to cut ties completely. To help you do this, I've written a prayer for you. Now, if you already understand your power and authority and you know how to pray, then by all means pray the prayer God leads you to pray. But this is here for those who may not know how yet — a guide to help you take your first stand, your first step of breaking agreement and stepping into freedom.

On the Other Side of Fear is Your Freedom

Prayer of Breaking Agreement with Anxiety

Father, in the name of Jesus, I come before You today and confess that I have, at times, agreed with anxiety—whether through fear, doubt, or believing lies that did not come from You. I repent for every silent agreement I have made that gave anxiety a place in my life. Right now, I break that partnership. Anxiety, you no longer have legal rights to my mind, my heart, or my future. I cancel every agreement I made with your lies, and I shut every door that I left open to you. Lord, I choose today to align myself with Your Word and Your truth. I put on the belt of truth and declare that Your promises are stronger than my feelings. I put on the breastplate of righteousness and thank You that I am covered by the finished work of Jesus. I take up the shield of faith to extinguish every fiery dart of fear. I place the helmet of salvation on my mind, and I speak peace over my thoughts. And I take up the sword of the Spirit, which is Your Word, and I will use it to silence every lie. From this moment forward, I declare that my agreement is with heaven. I walk in Your joy, Your peace, and Your confidence. Anxiety, you have been evicted, and the Word of God now rules in my heart. I belong to Jesus, and I stand in His authority. In Jesus name, I pray. **Amen.**

Anxiety doesn't come crashing in with signs of forced entry. It slips in quietly—through unchecked thoughts, hidden fears, moments of exhaustion, or the silence of isolation—until one day it feels like he's set up camp in your life. You may not have realized it at first, but by allowing him to stay, you gave him a kind of ownership. The good news is: what was allowed in can also be forced out. The first step is to take inventory. Sit with God and ask Him to show you what anxiety has stolen—your joy, your peace, your confidence. Naming the loss is the first step toward reclaiming it. Next, seal the cracks. Just like after a break-in, you secure the doors and windows. Spiritually, that means identifying the places where anxiety has gained access and closing them with truth, prayer, rest, and community. Then, suit up with the armor of God. You can't fight anxiety bare. God has equipped you with spiritual armor—truth, righteousness,

---

On the Other Side of Fear is Your Freedom

peace, faith, salvation, and His Word—to protect you and empower you to stand firm. Finally, pray with authority. Not timid prayers of fear, but bold declarations rooted in Scripture. Prayer activates your armor, breaks every agreement with anxiety, and aligns you with the promises of heaven. This chapter has shown you that anxiety doesn't own you—it only stays where it's allowed. You are spirit first, not feelings-driven. You have the authority in Christ to divorce anxiety, break covenant with it, and reclaim everything it has stolen. From this point forward, your agreement is no longer with fear but with God's truth. And when you align with heaven, victory is already yours.

CHAPTER Four

The Freedom Plan

Deliverance from anxiety isn't always instant. Overcoming anxiety God's way is not a quick fix—it's a transformation. It's the renewing of your mind, the reshaping of your heart, and the surrender of your will to His perfect plan. This process is not simply about *"feeling better."* It's about becoming new. When you begin this journey, you are going to shed the old systems of thinking—the lies you've believed, the fears you've nutured, and the patterns you've depended on for survival. Your flesh will not let go without a fight. Your body and mind have grown comfortable in these pattersn, even if they are destructive. They've been your *"normal."* In those moments your mind will scream, Go back! It will try to convince you that change is too hard, that GOD's promises are too far away, or that you aren't strong enough to finish this fight. This is when you must anchor yourself to the Word of God and stay the course. "Do not conform to the pattern of this world, but be transformed by the renewing of your mind..." *(Holy Bible, NIV, 2011, Romans 12:2)*. The transformation process will feel uncomfortable. Sometimes it will feel like you're losing your footing, but in reality, GOD is uprooting what was never meant to be planted in you. You are exchanging fear for faith, doubt for trust, and anxiety for peace. Think of it like this: anxiety has built a fortress in your life—brick by brick, lie by lie. When God begins His work, He doesn't just decorate the fortress; He tears it down and builds something entirely new. That tearing-down process is noisy, messy, and sometimes painful—but it's necessary. When your body resists, pray. When your mind doubts, declare the truth of God's Word out loud. When fear tries to creep back in, stand firm and remind yourself: I am being transformed. God is my strength. The old me is gone; the new me is being made in Christ. Every step of this transformation is proof that God is at work in you. And if you stay the course, even through the discomfort, you will not only overcome anxiety—you will walk in a new level of freedom you didn't know was possible. What does freedom look like for you? Picture it—your mind at peace, your heart steady, your spirit unshaken. No more sleepless nights gripped by fear. No more spirals of *"what if"* and *"I can't."* Freedom is living the life God already promised you—a life where His peace rules your mind and His joy strengthens your heart. You are in a fight right now. This is not just about surviving the day—it's about taking hold of the abundant life Jesus died to give you. The enemy will try to convince you that freedom is out of reach, but God says it's already yours. So I have to ask you: Are you ready? Can you see the life God has prepared for you? Are you willing to walk through the process? Are you up for the challenge? Let's go, Overcomer—because that's exactly who you are! This journey won't always be easy, but every step forward is a step into victory. You are not walking alone. God is with you, fighting for you, and shaping you into the warrior He created you to be. The transformation process is not just about what you leave behind—it's about intentionally stepping into what God has for you. Here's your roadmap:

Step 1: Surrender Completely

"Cast all your anxiety on Him because He cares for you"*(NIV, 1Peter 5:7)*.

You cannot carry anxiety and the peace of God at the same time. Begin by giving God full control of your life—including your thoughts, your fears, and your future. Speak it out loud:

On the Other Side of Fear is Your Freedom

"Lord, I give You my mind, my heart, and every anxious thought. I trust You with my life."

Step 2: Renew Your Mind Daily
"Do not conform to the pattern of this world, but be transformed by the renewing of your mind"*(NIV, Romans 12:2)*.

Replace lies with truth. When an anxious thought enters, confront it with Scripture. Example: If anxiety says, *"You're not safe,"* respond with Psalm 91:2, "...He is my refuge and my fortress, my God, in whom I trust"*(NIV, Psalms 91:2)*.

Daily practice:
- Read God's Word every morning.
- Write down at least one truth to meditate on throughout the day.

Step 3: Guard Your Heart and Mind
"Above all else, guard your heart, for everything you do flows from it."*(NIV, Proverbs 4:23)*. Be intentional about what you watch, listen to, and speak. Anxiety feeds on fear-filled, hopeless input. Protect your environment—fill it with worship, prayer, and encouragement.

Step 4: Pray Without Ceasing
"Do not be anxious about anything, but in every situation, by prayer and petition, with thanksgiving, present your requests to God"*(NIV, Philippians 4:6)*. Prayer is not your last resort—it's your first weapon. Turn every anxious thought into a prayer. Thank God in advance for the victory, even before you feel it.

Step 5: Walk in Faith, Not Feelings
"For we live by faith, not by sight"*(NIV, 2 Corinthians 5:7)*. Your feelings may scream fear, but faith says you are free. Choose to act based on God's Word, not your emotions. This may mean showing up, speaking up, or moving forward even when you feel afraid.

On the Other Side of Fear is Your Freedom

Step 6: Surround Yourself with Godly Support
"As iron sharpens iron, so one person sharpens another"(NIV, Proverbs 27:17). You were never meant to fight this battle alone. Find believers who will speak life into you, pray for you, and hold you accountable when you want to quit.

Step 7: Declare Your Victory Daily
"They triumphed over him by the blood of the Lamb and by the word of their testimony..."(NIV, Revelation 12:11). Your words carry power. Every day, speak life over yourself:

> *"I am free in Christ."*
> *"Fear has no hold on me."*
> *"The peace of God guards my heart and mind."*

Freedom isn't just possible—it's promised. God's Word says, *"Therefore if the Son makes you free, you shall be free indeed"(NKJV, John 8:36).* Stay the course, Overcomer. The life God has for you is worth every step of the fight. If you are going to be an overcomer, you must know it, believe it, and walk in it every day. From the very moment you open your eyes, your mindset matters. Throughout the night, God has been waging war on your behalf—fighting against every lie, fear, and scheme the enemy tried to plant in your mind. Anxiety will try to catch you off guard first thing in the morning—waiting to pounce on your words, your thoughts, and your focus. But you have a choice: to speak life, truth, and faith before anything else. Your first words are seeds. Plant the ones that align with God's promises, and you'll walk in the victory that He has already secured for you. Now lets take a look at the steps in greater detail.

Step 1: Surrender Completely
Surrender does not mean you give up or hand yourself over to anxiety's grip. It means you release your own tight hold on control—or more accurately, the illusion of control—so that God can step in.

On the Other Side of Fear is Your Freedom

We often try to calm our fears through control. We plan, micromanage, overanalyze, prepare for the worst. But control is a counterfeit comfort. It's anxiety's favorite disguise. God invites us to surrender. God will never force His way into your will. He is not an intruder; He is a responder. If you decide to keep holding hands with anxiety, He will allow it, because He honors your choice. But if you truly desire freedom, He will open that door. Surrender is an act of trust. It says, *"I cannot carry this, but I believe You can."* It is the conscious decision to stop wrestling in your own strength and to allow the One who spoke the universe into being to speak peace into your heart. Surrender stops us from trying to be our own savior, and reminds us that we already have one.

What This Looks Like in Practice

- **Admit your limits**— Acknowledge, *"I can't fix this in my own power."*

- **Release the need to control outcomes** — Stop micromanaging the *"what ifs"* and the *"how longs."*

- **Invite God in deliberately**— Through prayer, say, *"Lord, I give You full access to this space in my life."*

A Gentle Warning

Surrender is not a one-time checkbox. It's a repeated act, sometimes daily, sometimes minute-by-minute, especially when anxiety tries to creep back in. Each time, you return to that posture: *"Lord, it's Yours again."*

Reflective Exercise #1: Let Go

Sometimes surrender feels abstract—like a nice idea that's hard to actually do. That's why I want to give you something physical, something you can hold and release, to remind you what it means to truly let go. This isn't magic. The stone or object you choose has no power in itself. But when you use it as a symbol of the fears and worries you've been holding onto, it becomes a tool to help you practice surrender in a tangible way. As you open your hand and let it fall, you are making a conscious choice to release control and invite God's peace to take its place.

Purpose: To move surrender from the mind into the body, making it tangible.

What You'll Need: A small stone, coin, or any object you can hold in your hand.

Steps:

1. **Identify Your "Anxiety Object"**
   - Hold the stone (or object) in your hand.
   - As you grip it, think of the specific fears, worries, or situations that are weighing you down.

2. **Feel the Weight**
   - Notice how tightly you're holding it.
   - Recognize that this is how you've been clinging to the illusion of control.

3. **Pray the Prayer of Surrender**
   - While still holding the object, speak the prayer out loud: *"Father, I release my grip on these fears and invite You into this space…"*

4. **Physically Let Go**
   - Open your hand and drop the object into a bowl, basket, or even the ground.
   - As it leaves your hand, picture your anxiety leaving your heart and mind.

On the Other Side of Fear is Your Freedom

5. **Declare Your Freedom**
   - Say the Declaration of Freedom: *"Anxiety is not my master —*
   Jesus is…"

6. **Repeat as Needed**
   - Each time anxiety resurfaces, repeat this process. Over time, it becomes muscle memory for the soul.

Step 2: Renew Your Mind Daily
Renewing your mind is not a one-time event—it's a daily discipline. Anxiety thrives in mental clutter, lies, and rehearsed fears. But the Word of God is like fresh water to a thirsty soul, washing away toxic thoughts and replacing them with truth. One powerful truth about the mind lies in 2 Corinthians 10:5, where we are told to "…bringing every thought into captivity to the obedience of Christ" *(Holy Bible, NKJV, 1982, 2 Corithians 10:5)*. This means our thoughts are not free to roam unchecked. We are not helpless victims to whatever drifts into our minds. Instead, we have authority—through Christ—to hold each thought up against God's Word and decide if it can stay. If it aligns with truth, we keep it. If it does not, we cast it out immediately. We don't let it sit down, unpack its bags, and take root. This spiritual "thought arrest" is how we prevent anxiety from building a stronghold. Paul wrote, *"And do not be conformed to this world, but be transformed by the renewing of your mind…"* *(NKJV, Romans 12:2)*. Transformation happens one thought at a time, one day at a time.

When a thought *"takes root"* — whether positive or negative — it's not just a poetic metaphor. Scientifically, it's a real, physical process in the brain involving **neurons, synaptic connections,** and **neurochemistry.**

On the Other Side of Fear is Your Freedom

The Birth of a Thought
Every time you think something, a group of neurons (nerve cells) in your brain fire together in a pattern. This electrical firing triggers the release of chemicals called **neurotransmitters** (like dopamine, serotonin, glutamate) that allow neurons to "talk" to each other across small gaps called **synapses**.

Repetition Strengthens the Connection
The more you repeat a thought — whether it's "I'm safe in God's hands" or "I'm going to fail" — the stronger that neural pathway becomes. This is based on the principle "neurons that fire together, wire together" (Hebb's Law). Think of it like walking through tall grass:

- The first time you walk the path, it's barely visible.
- The more you walk it, the more trampled down and easy it is to follow.
- Eventually, it becomes the default path your brain takes.

Emotional Glue Locks It In
When a thought has a strong emotional charge (especially fear, anger, or joy), the brain's **amygdala** flags it as important. This signals the **hippocampus** (the brain's memory hub) to store the thought and its emotional context more deeply. That's why anxiety-triggering thoughts feel so *"sticky"* — they are literally reinforced by fear's chemical grip.

Habit Loops Form
Over time, repeated thoughts become **automatic** because the brain moves them from the conscious thinking centers (prefrontal cortex) into the more reflexive, habitual parts of the brain (basal ganglia). That's when they start *"running the show"* without you even realizing it.

On the Other Side of Fear is Your Freedom

The Good News: Neuroplasticity

The brain is *malleable* — a concept called **neuroplasticity**. Just as negative thoughts can carve deep grooves in your brain, **positive, truth-based thoughts** can form new pathways. If you stop walking the old *"fear"* path and start walking the *"faith"* path, the old one grows over, and the new one becomes dominant. This is why renewing your mind (NKJV, Romans 12:2) is not just spiritual truth — it's also brain science.

The Science of How Thoughts Take Root

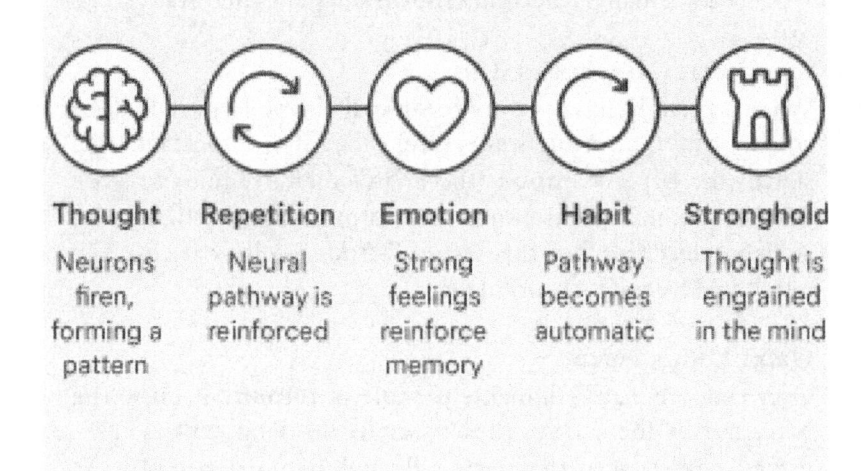

Thought	Repetition	Emotion	Habit	Stronghold
Neurons firen, forming a pattern	Neural pathway is reinforced	Strong feelings reinforce memory	Pathway becomes automatic	Thought is engrained in the mind

---

On the Other Side of Fear is Your Freedom

Thoughts affect **every part of your being**: mind, body, and soul — and science, Scripture, and lived experience all confirm this. Here's how they connect:

Mind — The Control Center
Your mind is where thoughts are born, shaped, and stored.

- **Spiritually**: Scripture says, "For as he thinks in his heart, so is he" *(NKJV, Proverbs 23:7)*. What you continually think shapes your beliefs, attitudes, and identity.
- **Scientifically**: Thoughts form neural pathways. Repeated thoughts strengthen those pathways, influencing how you interpret life and make decisions.

Body — The Physical Response
Thoughts trigger chemical and hormonal changes that affect your physical health.

- **Nervous System**: Anxiety-producing thoughts activate the **amygdala**, releasing stress hormones like cortisol and adrenaline.
- **Physical Symptoms**: These chemicals can raise heart rate, tighten muscles, cause stomach upset, and disrupt sleep.
- **Positive Thoughts**: Truth-based, hopeful thoughts can trigger dopamine and serotonin release, lowering stress and boosting immune function.

Soul — The Spiritual Core
The soul — your will, emotions, and inner life — is deeply influenced by what you dwell on.

- **Spiritually**: Philippians 4:8 urges believers to think on what is true, noble, right, pure, lovely, and praiseworthy *(KJV, Phillipians 4:8)*. When we fix our thoughts on these, our soul finds rest.
- **Emotionally**: Dwelling on fear or lies fuels inner unrest; dwelling on God's truth fosters peace, joy, and resilience.

On the Other Side of Fear is Your Freedom

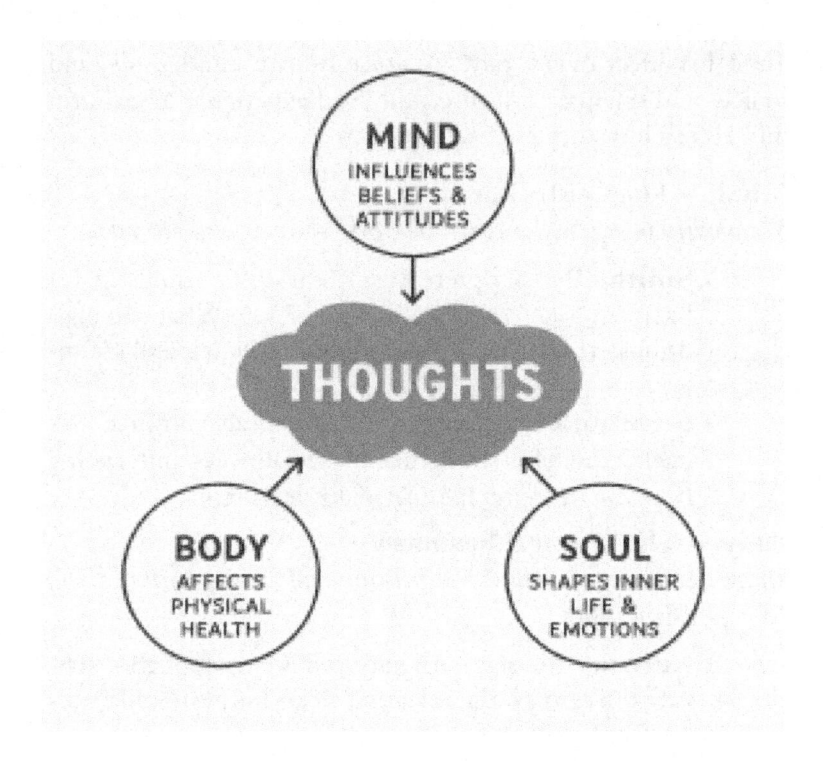

```
        MIND
    INFLUENCES
     BELIEFS &
     ATTITUDES
         ↓
      THOUGHTS
       ↑        ↖
    BODY        SOUL
   AFFECTS   SHAPES INNER
   PHYSICAL    LIFE &
    HEALTH    EMOTIONS
```

Reflective Exercise #2: Morning Reset

Each new day brings a flood of thoughts—some helpful, some harmful. Without realizing it, we often allow these thoughts to shape our moods, decisions, and view of ourselves. But God has given us a powerful tool: the ability to renew our minds through His truth. This exercise is designed to help you start and end your day grounded in Scripture, aware of your thought patterns, and equipped to choose truth over lies. Take a few quiet moments each morning to reset your focus, align your thoughts with God's Word, and walk in peace.

Purpose: To intentionally reset your mind each morning by anchoring your thoughts in Scripture, building spiritual awareness, and creating a habit of filtering daily thoughts through the lens of God's truth.

On the Other Side of Fear is Your Freedom

Reflection Questions:

- What *"old systems of thinking"* do I need to let go of today?
- How have I been resisting the transformation God wants to do in me?
- What does my promised life of freedom look like—and am I willing to fight for it?

Take a few moments to be still before the Lord. Let Him bring to light the lies you've believed, the fears you've carried, and the areas where you've settled for less than His best.

Steps:

1. **Choose a Verse** — Select one Scripture about peace, hope, or trust such as 2 Corinthians 10:5. Write it on a card or save it in your phone. *(NKJV, 2Corinthians 10:5)*.

2. **Read It Aloud**— Speak it over yourself when you wake up and before bed.

3. **Thought Checkpoint** — When a thought enters, stop and ask: Does this align with God's truth?

4. **Take Captive or Cast Out** — If it aligns, keep it. If it doesn't, verbally reject it: *"I cast this thought out in Jesus' name."*

5. **Repeat Daily** — Make this part of your daily mental routine until it becomes second nature.

On the Other Side of Fear is Your Freedom

Step 3: Guard Your Mind

In a world overflowing with noise, opinions, and constant demands on our attention, our hearts and minds are under siege. We are bombarded daily with messages that shape how we think, what we desire, and ultimately, who we become. The battle for peace, joy, and clarity is not fought on the outside—it's waged within. Guarding your heart and mind is not about living in fear or isolation; it's about intentional stewardship of your inner life. Scripture tells us that the heart is the wellspring of life and that the mind is renewed by truth. When we fail to protect these sacred places, the currents of culture, unfiltered emotions, and spiritual attacks can slowly erode our faith and stability. In this step, we'll explore how to stand watch over the gates of your soul, how to discern what you allow in, and how to partner with God's peace to keep you steady. You'll learn that guarding your heart is not about building walls, but about setting wise boundaries, filtering your influences, and nurturing the life God has placed within you. This is not just a defensive measure—it's a proactive way to live from a place of wholeness and strength.

The Scriptural Foundation

The instruction to *"guard your heart and mind"* is deeply rooted in Scripture. Two key verses frame this principle:

- **Proverbs 4:23** – "Above all else, guard your heart, for everything you do flows from it." This shows that the heart (biblically speaking—the seat of our thoughts, will, and emotions) determines the course of our lives *(NIV, Proverbs 4:23)*.
- **Philippians 4:6-7** – "Do not be anxious about anything, but in every situation, by prayer and petition, with thanksgiving, present your requests to God. And the peace of God, which transcends all understanding, will guard your hearts and your minds in Christ Jesus." Here,

---

On the Other Side of Fear is Your Freedom

the guarding is not just a self-effort—it's God's supernatural peace acting like a sentry over our inner life (NIV, Phillipians 4:6-7).

What It Means to "Guard"

In biblical times, the term *"guard"* paints the image of soldiers keeping watch over a city gate. Spiritually, it's the idea of being vigilant over what enters and influences your thoughts, emotions, and beliefs.

Practically, this includes:

- **Filtering Input:** Watching what you consume—whether through conversation, media, or relationships (NKJV, Psalm 101:3).
- **Challenging Thoughts:** Bringing every thought into obedience to Christ (NKJV, 2 Corinthians 10:5).
- **Staying Rooted in Truth:** Using Scripture as the standard for what is allowed to shape your mind (NKJV, John 17:17).

Guarding the Heart – The Inner Life

In Scripture, the *"heart"* encompasses more than feelings—it's your moral compass, your desires, and your spiritual center.

To guard the heart means:

- **Keeping it Pure:** "Blessed are the pure in heart, for they will see God" (NKJV, Matthew 5:8).
- **Aligning Desires with God's Will:** Delighting in Him so He shapes the desires of your heart (NKJV, Psalm 37:4).
- **Refusing Bitterness:** Not letting offense, unforgiveness, or cynicism take root (NKJV, Hebrews 12:15).

On the Other Side of Fear is Your Freedom

Guarding the Mind – The Battle of Thoughts

The mind is the battlefield where spiritual victories or defeats are often decided.

- To guard the mind means: **Renewing It Daily:** ..."Be transformed by the renewing of your mind"*(NIV, Romans 12:2)*.
- **Thinking on What's True**: Paul's list in Philippians 4:8—true, noble, right, pure, lovely, admirable—isn't a suggestion, it's a defense strategy *(NIV, Philipians 4:8)*.
- **Rejecting Lies**: Using God's Word to counter the enemy's deception *(NIV, Matthew 4:1-11)*.

God's Role vs. Our Role

Guarding is both our responsibility and God's promise.

- **Our Role:** Stay alert, stay in prayer, stay in the Word.
- **God's Role**: Provide supernatural peace and strength to keep us steady, even in trials.

Living This Out

You guard your heart and mind by:

- **Daily Time in God's Word** – The Word sharpens discernment.
- **Prayer and Worship** – These keep your focus on Him instead of circumstances.
- **Community** – Surround yourself with people who encourage your faith and speak life.
- **Boundaries–** Protect your spiritual health by saying no to influences that weaken you.

Being a watchman over what enters your heart and mind is vital to overcoming anxiety. Contrary to the old saying that *"words will never hurt us,"* both Scripture and life reveal that words carry power—in the spiritual realm and the natural. They can speak life or death, peace or unrest, faith or fear. Every thought, message, and influence you allow past the gates of your soul

---

On the Other Side of Fear is Your Freedom

shapes your inner reality. Left unguarded, these influences can plant seeds of doubt and anxiety. But when you intentionally choose what to let in and what to keep out, you create an environment where God's peace can flourish. Guarding your heart is more than a defensive measure —it is a daily partnership with God to preserve your joy, strengthen your faith, and walk in lasting freedom.

Reflective Exercise #3: The Gate of My Heart
This is a guided time of reflection that invites you to step into the role of a spiritual watchman over your inner life. Drawing from the biblical imagery of guarding the gates of a city, this exercise helps you examine the thoughts, influences, and emotions that shape your heart and mind. Through Scripture meditation, selfexamination, and intentional action, you will identify what strengthens your walk with God and what undermines it. This practice is not merely about protection—it is about cultivating a heart and mind where peace, purity, and truth can flourish.

Purpose: to help you slow down and take spiritual inventory of what you are allowing into your inner life. Just as ancient cities posted watchmen at their gates to control who entered, this exercise positions you as the watchman over your own heart and mind.

Steps:

1. Scripture Meditation (5-10 minutes)
Read slowly and prayerfully from your bible:

- **Proverbs 4:23** - "Above all else, guard your heart, for everything you do flows from it" *(NIV, Proverbs, 4:23).*
- **Philippians 4:6-7** - "The peace of God… will guard your hearts and your minds in Christ Jesus" *(NIV, Phillipians 4:6-7).*
- **Philippians 4:8** - "Think about such things…" *(NIV, Philippians 4:8).*

After reading, pause and imagine your heart and mind as a **city with gates**. God has called you to be the watchman.

On the Other Side of Fear is Your Freedom

2. Personal Reflection Questions

Write your responses in a journal or notebook:

A. What's Entering My Gates?
- What thoughts, media, conversations, or influences am I regularly letting in?
- Are they producing peace and life, or anxiety and compromise?

B. The Condition of My Heart
- Are there hidden areas of bitterness, fear, or discouragement I've ignored?
- What desires are driving my decisions lately—are they God-centered or self-centered?

C. Guard Posts I Need to Strengthen
- What boundaries or habits would help me guard my heart better?
- Who in my life encourages me toward God's truth and who distracts me from it?

D. Practical Action Step
- Pick **one influence** (a habit, media source, conversation, or thought pattern) that has been weakening your heart and mind.
- Commit to **closing that gate** for the next 7 days.
- Replace it with something that builds you spiritually (Scripture memory, uplifting worship, prayer walks, etc.).

3. Closing Prayer

Pray something like this:

Lord, I give You my heart and mind today. I ask You to help me be a faithful watchman over the gates of my soul. Remove anything that is not of You, and strengthen my desire for what is pure, noble, and true. Let Your peace guard me as I stay rooted in Christ. In Jesus' name, **Amen.**

On the Other Side of Fear is Your Freedom

Step 4: Pray Without Ceasing

Prayer is one of the most powerful weapons we have against the enemy. When we pray, we are not speaking into the air—we are inviting God Himself and the host of Heaven into our affairs. Prayer brings the authority, power, and resources of Heaven to earth, placing divine help and aid at your side. To overcome anxiety, prayer must become more than a momentary act— it must become the atmosphere you live in. Every whispered plea, every silent thought turned toward God, every grateful acknowledgment of His presence is an open door for His power to flood your situation. Prayer draws the line where anxiety loses its grip, because it shifts your focus from the weight of your problem to the greatness of your God. When you pray without ceasing, it becomes more than a habit—it becomes the rhythm of your life. Just as breathing sustains your body, prayer sustains your spirit. Every moment, every thought, every need is an opportunity to breathe out your concerns and breathe in His peace, wisdom, and strength. Over time, prayer stops being something you do only in crisis—it becomes the steady rhythm of a life anchored in God's presence. And in that place of continual communion, anxiety cannot take root, for your heart is guarded and your mind kept steady by the One who holds all things together. Prayer is as simple as talking with a friend. A healthy conversation is give and take—it's not one-sided. Don't be the friend who never lets the other person get a word in. When you pray, talk a little, then listen a little. God still speaks to His people. His voice isn't loud or forceful—it's a still, small voice that requires you to quiet your spirit and lean in *(NKJV, 1Kings 19:12)*. The more you make space to hear Him, the more you'll recognize His voice and the clearer His guidance will become. And don't just *"check the box"* when you pray. Prayer isn't a chore to complete—it's a relationship to deepen. Make the conversation meaningful, personal, and real. Even though you are going through your own struggles, remember—prayer is not all about you. When you pray for someone else, you shift your focus away from your own anxiety and struggles. Your prayers can become the lifeline someone else needs to make it through their day. It's important

---

On the Other Side of Fear is Your Freedom

to help others—not just in action, but also in prayer. Lifting up a friend, family member, or even someone you barely know can release compassion, break selfish patterns, and remind you that you're part of something bigger than yourself. Often, when you focus on helping someone else, you naturally spend less time dwelling on your own problems. And in the process, God often works on your heart and circumstances too.

How to Pray: A Simple Guide

1. Start with Worship and Praise
- Focus on who God is before anything else.
- "Enter his gates with thanksgiving and into his courts with praise" *(Holy Bible, KJV, 2017, Psalm 100:4).*

Example: *"Lord, I thank You for Your goodness and mercy."*

2. Confess and Surrender
- Clear the air—bring your sins and struggles honestly to Him.
- "If we confess our sins, he is faithful and just to forgive..." *(KJV, 1John 1:9).*

Example: *"Forgive me where I've fallen short. Help me walk in Your ways."*

3. Align with God's Will
- Invite His plan over yours.
- "Thy kingdom come, They will be done..."*(KJV, Matthew 6:10).*

Example: *"Lord, let Your will be done in my life today."*

4. Present Your Requests
- Bring your needs with trust, not fear.
- "...By prayer and petition, with thanksgiving, present your requests to God"(NIV, *Philippians* 4:6).

Example: *"I place my family, health, and future in Your hands."*

5. Listen for His Voice
- Pause. Quiet your heart and wait. Sometimes His answer comes as peace, Scripture, or a gentle nudge.
- "Be still, and know that I am God." *(KJV, Psalm 46:10).*

6. End with Thanksgiving and Faith
- Thank Him and trust His answer, even if you don't see it yet.
- "...If we ask anything according to His will, He hears us"(NKJV, *1John 5:14*).

Example: *"Thank You for hearing me, Lord. I trust You completely."*

This way, prayer isn't just a list you run through—it's a relationship you grow in. Talk a little, listen a little, and let God's voice guide your steps.

Understand the Heart of the Command
Paul's words in 1 Thessalonians 5:17 —"pray without ceasing"— doesn't mean abandoning your daily responsibilities to sit in a prayer closet 24/7. Instead, it's about cultivating a constant awareness of God's presence and maintaining an open, ongoing conversation with Him throughout the day (KJV, 1Thessalonians 5:17). Think of it less as one long prayer and more as a life lived in prayer.

On the Other Side of Fear is Your Freedom

Make Prayer the Atmosphere, Not Just an Event

- You can be talking with God while:
- Driving to work ("Lord, thank You for going ahead of me today.")
- Doing dishes ("God, help me serve my family with joy.")
- Walking into a meeting ("Holy Spirit, give me wisdom and peace.")
- Comforting your child ("Father, help me guide them with patience.")

These don't have to be long, formal prayers—just short, sincere moments that keep your heart connected.

Keep the Door of Your Heart Open

- When you leave the "door" open for God, you invite Him to:
- Interrupt your thoughts with His guidance.
- Redirect your emotions when anxiety or frustration rise.
- Remind you of His promises when you feel pressure.

This way, every moment becomes an opportunity for a divine exchange— you give Him your burdens, He gives you His peace.

Anchor Your Day with Intentional Touchpoints

While the goal is an ongoing connection, it helps to have set "check-ins" with God:

- **Morning:** Surrender the day before it starts.
- **Midday:** Pause to re-center and ask for renewed strength.
- **Evening:** Reflect and thank Him for His presence.

These moments train your heart to stay tuned to Him even while you're busy.

On the Other Side of Fear is Your Freedom

Live Aware, Not Distracted
Praying without ceasing is not about multitasking with God in the background—it's about living with Him in the foreground, even as you go about your work and care for your family. Over time, this habit transforms ordinary moments into holy ground and daily stress into steady peace.

Pray Without Ceasing in Daily Life
Practical ways to keep the door to God open—no matter how busy you are.

Morning Reset
- Before getting out of bed: "Lord, thank You for this day. Lead me in every step."
- Visualize placing your schedule, responsibilities, and emotions in His hands before your feet hit the floor.

Commute Conversations
- Turn off the news or music for part of your drive and talk to God.
- Pray over your workplace, coworkers, and any meetings or decisions ahead.

Chore Chats
- While cooking, folding laundry, or cleaning: thank God for your family, provision, and home.
- Ask Him to give you joy in serving through small tasks.

"Trigger" Prayers
Choose something you do often—checking your phone, washing your hands, opening your email—and make it a reminder to send up a quick prayer:
- "God, help me walk in wisdom."
- "Lord, give me patience and grace."

Parenting Moments
- When helping with homework: "God, give them clarity and confidence."
- When disciplining: "Lord, help me speak truth in love."

On the Other Side of Fear is Your Freedom

Midday Pause
- Stop for 60 seconds—close your eyes, breathe deep, and whisper: "I'm listening, Lord."
- Ask Him to reset your attitude and renew your strength.

Walking & Waiting
- Turn waiting in line, sitting in traffic, or walking to the restroom into micro-prayer moments.
- Pray for the person ahead of you, your neighbors, or a specific need.

Gratitude at Night
- As you lay down, review your day with God.
- Thank Him for His presence and confess any moments you drifted, asking Him to teach you from them.

Reflective Exercise #4: Keeping the Door Open

Keeping the door open means cultivating a posture of presence, where our spirit remains sensitive to His voice and our heart remains soft toward His correction, comfort, and love.

Purpose: To help you intentionally examine your daily life and discover ways to keep an open, ongoing connection with God—inviting Him into every moment as your source of peace, wisdom, and strength.

Scripture Meditation

Read and reflect on:

- **1 Thessalonians 5:16-18** - "Rejoice always, pray without ceasing, give thanks in all circumstances..."*(NIV, 1 Thessalonians 5:16-18).*
- **Philippians 4:6-7** - "...in every situation, by prayer and petition, with thanksgiving, present your requests to God. And the peace of God... will guard your hearts and your minds in Christ Jesus" *(NIV, Philippians 4:67).*

On the Other Side of Fear is Your Freedom

Write down one phrase from these verses that stands out to you and why.

Self-Reflection Questions

In a journal or notebook, prayerfully answer:

1. In what moments of my day do I naturally think about God?
2. Where do I tend to "close the door" and handle things on my own?
3. How does my current prayer life reflect trust—or anxiety?
4. What are the triggers in my day (tasks, emotions, interruptions) that could become invitations to pray?

Identify Your "Open-Door Moments"

List **three specific times** in your day when you could pause briefly to invite God in—while working, parenting, commuting, cooking, or resting. Write a short prayer you could pray in each of those moments. When anxiety, shame, or distraction try to close the door, it's easy to assume God has stepped away. But He hasn't moved—we have. Keeping the door open means cultivating a posture of presence, where our spirit remains sensitive to His voice and our heart remains soft toward His correction, comfort, and love.

Example:

- **Morning coffee** - *"Lord, lead my thoughts before my day begins."*
- **Walking to a meeting** - *"God, give me clarity and peace."*
- **Tucking in my children** - *"Bless and protect them as they rest."*

On the Other Side of Fear is Your Freedom

Daily Commitment
For the next 7 days, intentionally practice keeping the door open to God in those three moments. Use a journal or phone notes to jot down how it changes your peace, mood, or perspective.

Closing Prayer
Lord, help me to live with my heart always open to You. Teach me to invite You into the ordinary, to hear Your whisper in the middle of my busyness, and to receive Your peace in the midst of life's demands. Let prayer become my constant rhythm, my steady breath, and my unbroken lifeline to You. **Amen.**

Step 5: Walk in Faith, Not Feelings
Faith is a choice, not a mood. Feelings are like the weather—they can change by the hour. Faith, however, is a decision to trust God's truth regardless of the emotional forecast. If we anchor our spiritual walk to feelings, we'll drift with every gust of anxiety, doubt, or discouragement. Faith says, *"I will act on what God has said, even when my emotions argue otherwise."* Anxiety is a spiritual entity—one that thrives on chaos—it will exploit emotional instability. It whispers, *"You don't feel peaceful, so God must not be with you."* But feelings are not proof of God's absence or presence. Walking in faith shuts the door on anxiety's favorite tactic: using temporary emotions to make you doubt eternal truths. Imagine you're hiking a mountain trail at dawn. You know the summit holds a breathtaking view, but halfway up, a heavy fog rolls in. The trail blurs, shadows stretch strangely, and your mind starts whispering, What if you're lost? What if there's danger ahead? Your heart races, and your body wants to turn back. But then you remember—the map in your hand, given to you by someone who's been here before, is still accurate. The path hasn't changed just because you can't see it clearly. So you take the next step. Then another. You trust the map more than you trust the fog. Eventually, the mist thins, and the light breaks through. Walking in faith is like that—choosing to keep moving toward God's promises, even when your feelings tell you you're lost. The fog of anxiety doesn't erase the truth; it

---

On the Other Side of Fear is Your Freedom

just tries to hide it. Your job is to follow the Mapmaker, not your momentary emotions.

Biblical Picture

- **Peter Walking on Water** – Peter began in faith, stepping out of the boat. But when he looked at the waves (circumstances) and felt fear (emotion), he started to sink. The lesson? Keep your eyes on the One who called you, not the waves that surround you *(NKJV, Matthew 14:22-33)*.
- **2 Corinthians 5:7** – "For we walk by faith, not by sight." We could paraphrase: We walk by faith, not by feelings *(NKJV, 2Corithians 5:7)*.

Spiritual Posture

Think of faith as your spiritual compass. Emotions might cloud the sky, but the compass always points to true north. Even in a storm, faith will direct your steps toward safety. The more consistently you choose faith over feelings, the weaker anxiety's grip becomes.

1. Recognize anxiety's voice for what it is.

Anxiety often exaggerates, jumps to worst-case scenarios, and ignores God's promises. When you notice those thoughts, name them for what they are: *"This is fear talking, not truth."*

- Remember, God has not given you a spirit of fear, but of power, love, and a sound mind *(NKJV, 2Timothy 1:7)*.

2. Replace the lies with God's truth.

Once you've identified the lies, replace them with God's truth.

- When anxiety says, *"You can't handle this,"* answer with Philippians 4:13— "I can do all things through Christ who strengthens me" *(NKJV, Philippians 4:13)*.

- When it says, *"God has abandoned you,"* declare Deuteronomy 31:6— "The Lord your God goes with you; He will never leave you nor forsake you"*(NKJV, Deuteronomy 31:6)*.

On the Other Side of Fear is Your Freedom

Keep a *"truth list"* handy with verses you can read out loud when panic rises.

3. Bring your anxiety to God immediately.

Faith doesn't mean pretending you're not anxious — it means taking that anxiety to Him before it grows in your mind. Pray honestly: *"Lord, my thoughts feel out of control, but I trust You to hold me and guide me through this."*

- Philippians 4:6-7 promises that **God's peace will guard your heart and mind** when you pray instead of worrying *(NKJV, Philippians 4:6-7).*

4. Worship while you wait for peace.

Anxiety often keeps your attention on *"what's wrong,"* but worship redirects your focus to the One who is right and in control. Play worship music, sing, or speak praise out loud — even if you don't feel like it. **Praise is a faith act** that pushes back the noise of fear.

5. Take one step of faith at a time.

Faith is not about feeling brave; it's about moving forward with God in spite of fear. Ask yourself, *"What's one small thing I can do right now in obedience to God?"* Then do it. Over time, these steps build trust and weaken anxiety's grip.

On the Other Side of Fear is Your Freedom

Reflective Exercise #5: Truth Over Anxiety

Anxiety has a voice – one that often shouts worst-case scenarios, distorts reality, and drowns out the promises of God. But as believers, we are called to recognize that voice for what it is: fear, not truth. This exercise is designed to help you identify anxiety's lies, replace them with the life-giving truth of Scripture, and take intentional steps of faith even when fear is present. Through reflection, prayer, worship, and action, you will practice shifting your focus from what's wrong to the One who is right and in control. Over time, these habits strengthen trust in God, weaken anxiety's grip, and train your heart to respond to fear with unwavering faith.

Purpose: To intentionally recognize anxiety's lies, replace them with God's truth, and take steps of faith while inviting God's peace into your heart.

Step 1 — Recognize Anxiety's Voice

1. Think about a recent moment when anxiety spoke loudly in your mind.
2. Write down the thoughts exactly as they came.
3. Next to each thought, write: "This is fear talking, not truth."
4. Read 2 Timothy 1:7 out loud: "For God has not given us the spirit of fear, but of power, and of love, and a sound mind" *(KJV, 2 Timothy 1:7).*
5. Reflect: How does this verse shift how you see that anxious thought?

Step 2 — Replace the Lies with God's Truth

1. Identify one lie anxiety told you today.
2. Find a matching Scripture from your "truth list" to counter it. For example:
    - Lie: *"I can't handle this."*
    - Truth: *"I can do all things through Christ who strengthens me"*
3. Write out the Scripture and personalize it with your name.

On the Other Side of Fear is Your Freedom

Step 3 — Bring Your Anxiety to God Immediately

1. Pause right now and pray honestly: *"Lord, my thoughts feel out of control, but I trust You to hold me and guide me through this."*
2. Journal one sentence about how you want God to help you in this situation.
3. Read Philippians 4:6-7 (NKJV) and underline the promise about peace.

Step 4 — Worship While You Wait

1. Choose one worship song that lifts your heart toward God.
2. Play it and either sing along or speak the lyrics out loud.
3. Write one sentence describing how worship changed your focus.

Step 5 — Take One Step of Faith

1. Ask yourself: *"What's one small thing I can do right now in obedience to God?"*
2. Write it down and commit to doing it today.
3. End by declaring out loud: *"Faith is not the absence of fear — it's the decision to lean on God's truth when fear is present."*

Step 6: Surround Yourself with Godly Support

Society tells us that we are individuals and that we must do it on our own. We live in a world where doing it alone is celebrated. Everything is about self this and self that — self-care, self-love, self-reliance. But GOD tells us in His Word that we are all a part of one body, just like Jesus, GOD the Father, and the Holy Spirit. We are joined fitly together. When one falls, we all fall. GOD was telling us that we need each other. GOD says to love the Lord your God with all your heart, with all your mind, and with all your soul, and then He says love your neighbor as yourself. On these two hang all the law and the prophets. There is nothing about this that says *"stand alone."* In isolation, anxiety does its best work. In isolation, anxiety is often unchecked. Godly support does not just happen at church. In fact, most often the support you need will come from the community you have created. And if you haven't created one, I am here to tell you that you will need someone to overcome anxiety. During my worst panic attacks, I had to call somebody. In my worst moments, I had to reach out for prayer. Godly support looks like brothers and sisters in Christ who will remind you of His promises, speak truth when your mind is clouded, and hold you up when you feel too weak to stand. Ecclesiastes 4:9-10— "Two are better than one, because they have a good return for their labor: If either of them falls down, one can help the other up"*(NIV, Ecclesiastes 4:9-10).* Hebrews 10:24-25 — "Let us consider how we may spur one another on toward love and good deeds... encouraging one another— and all the more as you see the Day approaching" *(NIV, Hebrews 10:24-25).*

On the Other Side of Fear is Your Freedom

Reflective Exercise #6: Surround Yourself with Godly Support

Anxiety feeds on isolation, but faith grows in community. God designed us to walk through life together – lifting each other up, speaking truth in love, and standing shoulder-to-shoulder in prayer. This reflective exercise will help you take an honest look at your support system, strengthen the relationships God has already placed in your life, and intentionally build new ones that will help you stand firm when fear tries to pull you away. As you walk through these steps, you'll discover that godly support isn't a luxury for difficult times – it's a lifeline that keeps your faith steady every day.

Purpose: To help you identify, strengthen, and intentionally build relationships that point you back to God when anxiety tries to isolate you.

1. Reflect on Your Circle
- List three people who encourage you in your faith.
- Next to each name, write one way they've helped you see God's truth when you felt overwhelmed.

2. Strengthen Your Support
- Choose one person from your list to connect with this week.
- Schedule a coffee, phone call, or prayer time.
- Pray: "Lord, help me nurture relationships that honor You and strengthen my faith."

3. Seek Accountability
- Identify one area where anxiety tends to take hold.
- Ask a trusted believer to check in with you regularly and pray with you about it.

On the Other Side of Fear is Your Freedom

4. Build New Connections
- If you feel your circle is small, join a Bible study, prayer group, or Christian community where you can be both encouraged and an encourager.
- Write one step you can take this month to expand your support network.

5. Anchor in Scripture
- Read **Ecclesiastes 4:9-10** and journal what it means for you personally to "help one another up"*(NIV, Ecclesiastes 4:9-10)*.
- Read **Hebrews 10:24-25** and write one way you can "spur someone on toward love and good deeds" this week *(NIV, Hebrews 1:24-25)*.

Godly support is a two-way street. The more you invest in encouraging others, the more your own faith will grow — and the less space anxiety will have to speak.

On the Other Side of Fear is Your Freedom

Step 7: Declare Your Victory Daily

Victory over anxiety is not a one-time moment—it is a daily decision to stand on God's promises no matter what you feel. The enemy will try to whisper fear into your heart, but you have the authority in Christ to speak truth louder than those lies. Declaring victory is not about denying your struggles; it's about choosing to see yourself as God sees you—already more than a conqueror through Christ. Every day, your words have power. Proverbs 18:21 reminds us that "The tongue has the power of life and death..." *(NIV, Proverbs 18:21)*. Speaking God's Word over your life strengthens your faith, shifts your focus from fear to hope, and reminds the enemy that he has no hold on you. This isn't about positive thinking, it's about biblical truth-speaking. When you declare God's Word, you are agreeing with Heaven's reality over your earthly situation. You are reminding your heart of His faithfulness, your mind of His promises, and your spirit of His victory.

- **Romans 8:37** — "...In all these things we are more than conquerors through Him who loved us"*(NIV, Romans 8:37)*.

- **1 Corinthians 15:57** — "But thanks be to God! He gives us the victory through our Lord Jesus Christ"*(NIV, 1Corithians 15:57)*.

- **Isaiah 54:17** — "No weapon forged against you will prevail, and you will refute every tongue that accuses you" *(NIV, Isaiah 54:17)*.

- **Job 22:28** —The Bible tells us, "Thou shalt also decree a thing, and it shall be established unto thee:..."*(KJV, Job 22:28)*.

Our words carry weight— not just because they sound good, but because they are rooted in spiritual authority. Too often, we underestimate this truth because we see life through our humanity instead of our spirit. Yet our God framed the world with His words, and that same creative power lives within us. Our words

---

On the Other Side of Fear is Your Freedom

are either building faith or feeding fear. If you are defeated in your mind, you will most likely speak defeat. If you are victorious in your mind, you will speak victory. This is why Scripture calls us to be "...transformed by the renewing of your mind..." *(NKJV, Romans 12:2)*. Renewing your mind daily removes old patterns of thinking, bad habits, and the residue of yesterday's pain or trauma. It creates space for truth, faith, and hope to rise—so your words align with God's promises instead of your fears. Victory declarations are not wishful thinking, they are faith-filled agreements with what God has already said. And when you speak what God speaks, you release His truth into your situation.

Victory Declaration Plan

I created a 31-day Victory Declaration Plan to help guide you on your journey, but before we go further, I need to share a confession. Just a few days ago, I lost my job. When Monday morning came, I tried to begin my day in prayer, yet I couldn't seem to find my footing. A wave of fear pressed in on me, and I knew that if I had pushed through in prayer, I could have resisted the enemy's attack. Instead, I found myself weighed down, not only by my own thoughts, but also by the worry I saw in my husband's eyes. His concern stirred up my own, even though deep down I believe this loss is a divine setup—God making space for me to finish this book. For a moment, I hesitated to admit this. After all, I am writing about deliverance, and yet here I am still wrestling from time to time. But God reminded me of something important: anxiety is not just a feeling, it is a spirit. And when we do not rise each morning clothed in prayer and covered in His promises, we leave an opening for that spirit to slip in. Deliverance is not the absence of battle; it is learning to fight daily from a place of victory. This is the truth I want you to hold on to: even after the house has been swept clean, anxiety will try to return, looking for a foothold. But this is not failure—it is the nature of the fight. Our part is to stay consistent, to put on the armor of God before the day begins, and to remind ourselves

---

On the Other Side of Fear is Your Freedom

of His Word when the enemy whispers lies. Some days we may stumble, but His strength always meets us there. Deliverance is not about never struggling again; it is about knowing where to run, who to call on, and how to rise up each time the battle comes. This is a daily fight—but one in which victory is already promised. The enemy tried to convince me that by sharing my struggles, I would lose credibility—that I could never be seen as an "expert." And you know what? He's right. I am not an expert. I am simply someone walking through this journey, leaning on God, and sharing honestly how He brings me through. I still fall. I am not perfect. Perfection belongs to God alone. My responsibility is not to present myself as flawless, but to testify of His goodness, to share my story, and to proclaim His truth so that others can find freedom too. The reality is that over forty million people live with some form of anxiety, and that is no small thing. I pray with everything in me that God will use this book to bring freedom to countless lives. Yes, the enemy whispers that this work will not amount to much, that no one will read it, and that even if they do, it will not be impactful. But I refuse to accept those lies. Instead, I choose to believe the Word of my Father in Heaven, my Lord and Savior Jesus Christ. The enemy never fights against what has no value. If he is fighting you, it is because he has seen your future. He knows the greatness God has already written into your story. He knows your latter days are destined to be greater than your former. He knows he has no place in what God is preparing, so he tries to delay what Heaven has already established. But he cannot undo what God has decreed. So walk boldly in the victory that is guaranteed to you as a believer. The enemy knows you will amount to something—and so do I. Do not shrink back. Do not let fear dictate your future. Walk in victory, and be great.

On the Other Side of Fear is Your Freedom

Reflective Exercise #7: 31-Day Victory Declaration Plan

Each morning, declare at least three victory statements from Scripture out loud. Each night, thank God for victories — no matter how small — that you saw that day. Over time, you'll train your mind and spirit to walk in victory as your default posture.

Day 1: I am fearfully and wonderfully made *(NIV, Psalm 139:14).*

Day 2: I have the mind of Christ *(NIV, 1 Corinthians 2:16).*

Day 3: I am more than a conqueror through Him who loves me *(NIV, Romans 8:37).*

Day 4: The Lord is my shepherd; I lack nothing *(NIV, Psalm 23:1).*

Day 5: God's peace guards my heart and mind *(NIV, Philippians 4:7)*

Day 6: No weapon formed against me will prosper *(NIV, Isaiah 54:17)*

Day 7: The joy of the Lord is my strength *(NIV, Nehemiah 8:10)*

Day 8: God's grace is sufficient for me, and His power is made perfect in my weakness *(NIV, 2 Corinthians 12:9).*

Day 9: I am chosen, holy, and dearly loved *(NIV, Colossians 3:12).*

Day 10: I am free from fear, for God has given me power, love, and a sound mind *(NIV, 2 Timothy 1:7).*

Day 11: I am the righteousness of God in Christ *(NIV, 2 Corinthians 5:21).*

Day 12: The Lord is my refuge and fortress; I trust Him *(NIV, Psalm 91:2).*

On the Other Side of Fear is Your Freedom

Day 13: God is working all things together for my good *(NIV, Romans 8:28).*

Day 14: I can do all things through Christ who strengthens me *(NIV, Philippians 4:13).*

Day 15: The Lord goes before me and will never leave me *(NIV, Deuteronomy 31:8).*

Day 16: I walk by faith, not by sight *(NIV, 2 Corinthians 5:7).*

Day 17: I am healed by the stripes of Jesus *(NIV, Isaiah 53:5).*

Day 18: God's favor surrounds me like a shield *(NIV, Psalm 5:12).*

Day 19: I am God's workmanship, created for good works *(NIV, Ephesians 2:10).*

Day 20: Greater is He who is in me than he who is in the world *(NIV, 1 John 4:4).*

Day 21: My steps are ordered by the Lord *(NIV, Psalm 37:23).*

Day 22: When anxiety was great within me, Your consolation brought me joy" *(NIV, Psalm 94:19).*

Day 23: I am strong in the Lord and in His mighty power *(NIV, Ephesians 6:10)*

Day 24: The Lord will fight for me; I need only to be still *(NIV, Exodus 14:14).*

Day 25: God has plans to prosper me and not to harm me, to give me hope and a future *(NIV, Jeremiah 29:11).*

Day 26: I am an overcomer by the blood of the Lamb and the word of my testimony *(NIV, Revelation 12:11).*

Day 27: The Spirit of the Lord is upon me; He has anointed me for His work *(NIV, Luke 4:18).*

Day 28: I have the strength for today and bright hope for tomorrow *(NIV, Lamentations 3:22–23).*

On the Other Side of Fear is Your Freedom

Day 29: I cast all my cares on Him because He cares for me *(NIV, 1Peter 5:7)*.

Day 30: My heart is steadfast, trusting in the Lord *(NIV, Psalm 112:7)*.

Day 31: Thanks be to God, who gives me the victory through my Lord Jesus Christ *(NIV, 1Corinthians 15:57)*.

What if you fail at all the steps? What if you forget to surrender, let anxious thoughts run wild, skip prayer, and find yourself walking in fear instead of faith? The good news is this: failure does not disqualify you. God already knew the moments you would stumble, and His grace covers them all. The fight against anxiety isn't about perfection—it's about persistence. When you fall, the most important thing you can do is get back up and return to God. Repent, realign, and restart. His mercies are new every morning, and even when you feel weak, He remains strong. The enemy wants you to believe that messing up means it's over—but that's a lie. Falling short simply reminds us that we cannot do this in our own strength; we need Him every single day. So when you fail, don't run from God—run to Him. Put your armor back on, declare His promises again, and step forward knowing that deliverance is not about never struggling, but about always choosing to rise up through His power. Remember, I stumbled while writing this very chapter— but I didn't stop, and neither should you. The enemy wants you to believe that a fall is final, but he is a liar. Failure is not final unless you choose to stay down. Get up, shake it off, keep going, keep pressing, keep surrendering, because you are more than what anxiety tries to tell you. You are not defeated- you are an Overcomer. Every time you rise, you remind hell that it has no claim on your life. So lift your head, square your shoulders, and walk forward in the victory that already belongs to you. Let's go, Overcomer—because that is who you are, and nothing can change it.

On the Other Side of Fear is Your Freedom

The primary types of anxiety disorders

- **Generalized Anxiety Disorder** (GAD) characterized by excessive worry
- **Panic Disorder** involving sudden and intense panic attacks
- **Social Anxiety Disorder** marked by intense fear of social situations
- **Specific Phobias** which are extreme fears of specific objects or situations
- **Separation Anxiety Disorder** involving excessive fear of being away from a loved one
- **Agoraphobia** a fear of situations where escape may be difficult
- **Selective Mutism** a persistent failure to speak in specific situations

CHAPTER Five

GOD + Therapy

I didn't see it coming. One moment I was fine, and the next, I was gasping for air, heart racing, mind spinning out of control. My first panic attack hit me like a wave I couldn't swim out of. I prayed—oh, how I prayed. I begged God to take it away, to calm my heart, to bring peace to my thoughts. But nothing seemed to change. It wasn't that my prayers weren't working— it was that I didn't understand what was happening to me, or even what to pray for. How do you fight an enemy you can't name? How do you ask God to heal something you don't fully understand? God is the Great Physician, the One who sees every wound—both visible and invisible. He knows the root of our pain before we can name it, and He offers healing that goes deeper than anything this world can give. But often, God also uses earthly vessels to carry His wisdom into our lives. That's where therapy comes in. Therapy is not a lack of faith—it's a tool God can use to answer the very prayers you've prayed. The same God who can heal in an instant can also choose to walk you through a process, using trained professionals to help you uncover the lies you've believed, the patterns you've formed, and the triggers you've ignored. God renews your spirit; therapy helps your mind to live in that renewal. Together, they don't compete—they complete the work of healing. That's when I learned something that would change the way I approached my healing: God and therapy work together. Therapy helps you work through things, and God is the one who shows you what's been hiding in the dark. Sometimes you just need someone else—a trained eye—to point out the missing piece, the root cause, the thing lurking in the background. When God's truth and therapy's tools meet, it's a one-two punch. God renews your spirit; therapy helps you untangle your thoughts. God grants peace; therapy empowers you to maintain it. Together, they address the mind, the soul, and the body—making you not just a survivor, but a conqueror. More than 40 million people live with some form of anxiety every single day. Some have walked through church doors seeking freedom, only to leave still carrying the weight. Others have tried therapy, only to grow discouraged and give up. One thing is certain: God can deliver and heal in an instant. But for some of us, anxiety has become so intertwined with our daily lives that we don't even hand it over to Him. We clutch it—sometimes without realizing it—because it has woven itself into how we think, feel, and function. That's when we need someone to ride with us as we navigate the road to deliverance and healing. Someone to remind us of the turns we can't see, the blind spots we've missed, and the truth that we can arrive at peace. God is at the wheel, but therapy helps us quiet the urge to reach over in panic and instead trust His perfect navigation."How can two walk together, except they be agreed"*(Holy Bible, NIV, 2011, Amos 3:3)*. When it comes to therapy, this truth matters. You need a therapist you can trust—someone whose approach aligns with your values and your needs. If you go to a session and it's not a good fit, that's okay. Find another one. Just because the first (or second) therapist isn't right for you doesn't mean therapy doesn't work. It simply means you haven't found your person yet. For far too long, we've treated therapy as a last resort—something *"only crazy people"* need. That mindset has kept many from even trying, and when they do finally go, they feel ashamed. There's still a cloud of stigma hanging over the idea of sitting down with a counselor. You cannot let the opinions of others determine the course of your healing. If it bothers you that much, you don't have to tell anyone. And even if they do find out, so what? Which is more important—their opinion, or your freedom? I admonish you to choose the latter. People are fickle. Their opinions shift like the wind. If you live to please them, you'll find yourself tossed back and forth, never settling into peace. But this journey—your journey—is about you. It's about wellness, deliverance, and healing. It's about becoming whole, no matter who understands it or who doesn't. Anxiety is one of those struggles that many people don't truly understand unless they've experienced it themselves. To outsiders, it may look like simple stress or worry, but for those who live with it, anxiety can feel like an overwhelming storm that refuses to quiet down no matter how hard you try. People often think they know what it is, but the reality runs much deeper. When facing anxiety, it's easy to search for quick fixes or lean on methods that only ease the symptoms for a moment. Therapy can be a helpful tool—a vehicle that provides strategies and perspective—but it isn't the final answer. The lasting calm we long for doesn't come from therapy alone; it comes from God. True healing and freedom are found in trusting Him, laying our worries at His feet, and letting His presence quiet the storms within. Until I began having panic attacks, the only time I had ever encountered a counselor was back in middle school. When the attacks started happening more frequently, I realized I couldn't handle it alone and needed help. That's when I scheduled a virtual appointment with a VA counselor. The day of my first session, I was nervous and tried to limit what I shared—but she saw right through me. As she gently began to unpack what I had been carrying, everything came tumbling out. The emotional floodgates opened, and I cried through the entire appointment. By the time the hour was up, I felt lighter, like a huge weight had been lifted off my shoulders. She didn't leave me on my own after that. She gave me homework, resources, and websites to help me better understand what I was dealing with and taught me techniques to begin overcoming it. I loved the virtual sessions because I was in the comfort of my own space, and I didn't have to walk back through a lobby feeling exposed or embarrassed.

On the Other Side of Fear is Your Freedom

It just worked for me. My husband questioned whether virtual appointments could be effective, believing in-person sessions were the only way. But I didn't agree. The truth is, the journey is about what works for you—not what others think should work. For me, virtual counseling was a Godsend. With each session, I grew stronger and found myself looking forward to sharing my progress. I know I was blessed to connect with the right counselor on the very first try, but that isn't always the case. Sometimes it takes meeting with a few different counselors before you find the one who truly fits and aligns with your values. At the same time, going back to church gave me an even deeper foundation. Not only was I equipped with practical tools and knowledge, but I was also armed with the Word of God. My faith sharpened my sword, teaching me how to use it in the battle against anxiety. All the techniques in the world would not have helped me if I didn't have the Word of God standing beside me. I had always carried a normal fear of death, but that fear deepened and shifted after my father and sister passed away within just months of each other. Up until then, death was something that always seemed to happen to other people. Suddenly, I found myself thinking, I must be next. One day, while flying home from visiting family, I decided to open my Bible on the plane. I hate flying too, so this impromptu Bible study served a dual purpose: calming my nerves and feeding my spirit. As I flipped through familiar passages, I came across John 14:1-4: "Let not your heart be troubled: ye believe in God, believe also in Me. In my Father's house are many mansions: if it were not so, I would have told you. I go to prepare a place for you. And if I go and prepare a place for you, I will come again, and receive you unto Myself; that where I am, there ye may be also" *(Holy Bible, KJV, 2017, John 14:1-4)*. The moment I read those verses, my eyes filled with tears. The Holy Spirit overshadowed me, and I could barely contain myself. I had to cover my mouth tightly to keep from disturbing the other passengers as I cried until the plane landed. Those words washed over me and I had a breakthrough. I realized that no matter what happened, Jesus had already made a place for me. That truth erased the fear of leaving this earth. Now, I'm not saying I'm ready to go today—but I know when the time comes, it won't be by accident. Death comes to everyone. The difference is, I now know that Jesus has always had me in mind. He prepared a place specifically for me. That truth built a shield around my spirit. When fear and anxiety tried to show up again, they just bounced off me. It was as if God Himself created an impenetrable force field around me, and they couldn't touch me. That moment on the plane remains one of the most powerful encounters I've ever had with God. He fought for me, and I know He will fight for you too.

Why Therapy Can Work Alongside God's Word
God's Word is complete, powerful, and able to transform lives on its own *(Holy Bible, NKJV, 1982, 2Timothy 3:16-17)*. God Himself is our ultimate healer, comforter, and counselor (NKJV, Psalm 34:18, Isaiah 9:6). However, going to therapy doesn't mean replacing or doubting God's power—it can be one of the ways God works in our healing process.

God Often Uses People as Part of His Healing Process
Throughout the Bible, God used human help to accomplish His purposes. Moses had Aaron to speak for him. Paul had Luke, a physician. Even the Good Samaritan used oil, bandages, and practical care for the wounded man. Therapists can be part of that help—using wisdom, listening, and skills to guide someone through struggles.

Therapy Is Not a Replacement for God's Word
Therapy doesn't take God's place; it can help you understand how your mind, body, and emotions work so you can better apply God's truth. For example, you might know Philippians 4:6-7 says "...do not be anxious,..." but a therapist can help you uncover why anxiety is triggered and teach ways to respond biblically *(NKJV, Philippians 4:6-7)*.

On the Other Side of Fear is Your Freedom

God Created Minds That Can Learn and Heal

God gave people the ability to study human behavior, brain function, and emotional health. Just as we go to a doctor for a broken bone, we can go to a counselor for emotional wounds—still trusting God as our ultimate healer.

The Key Is the Source of Counsel

Proverbs 11:14 says, "Where no counsel is, the people fall: But in the multitude of counselors there is safety." The safest therapy is rooted in biblical truth. A Christian therapist can offer both professional wisdom and God's Word. Even if a therapist isn't Christian, you can filter their guidance through Scripture *(Holy Bible, KJV, 2017, Proverbs 11:14)*.

Bottom line: We go to therapy not because God is lacking, but because He often works through people to bring wisdom, perspective, and healing. God's Word is the foundation, but therapy can be a tool that helps us live it out more effectively.

Questions to Ask Before Choosing a Therapist

Faith & Beliefs
- Do you incorporate faith into your counseling approach?
- Are you comfortable using Scripture and prayer in sessions if I request it?
- What is your personal view on God, the Bible, and Christian values?

Why it matters: You want a counselor who either shares your faith or respects it deeply so their guidance won't contradict God's Word.

On the Other Side of Fear is Your Freedom

Alignment With Biblical Values
- How do you handle situations where your advice might differ from my beliefs?
- What is your stance on marriage, forgiveness, and moral decision-making?
- Do you believe absolute truth exists, and if so, how do you define it?

Why it matters: God's Word should remain your ultimate authority, not the therapist's opinion.

Approach & Techniques
- What counseling methods or techniques do you use?
- How do you address anxiety, depression, or trauma in a faith-sensitive way?
- Will you give me practical tools I can apply alongside prayer and Scripture?

Why it matters: Some techniques are neutral or helpful, while others may conflict with biblical truth.

- Are you comfortable if I decline guidance that conflicts with my faith?

Why it matters: A good therapist will honor your spiritual convictions and not push you toward choices that compromise them.

Credentials & Experience
- Do you have experience working with Christians or church communities?
- Are you licensed and trained in addressing both emotional and spiritual concerns?

Why it matters: Professional skill and biblical sensitivity together make for the best support.

On the Other Side of Fear is Your Freedom

A good counselor honors your belief system, uncovers the places that are broken, and walks with you toward healing. A good counselor doesn't come to tear down your beliefs or demand that you start over. Instead, they honor the framework of faith and values that already shapes who you are. They recognize that your belief system is not something to be discarded but a foundation that, when cared for, can support your healing. Within that framework, however, a counselor also helps you see what you may not have noticed. They shine a gentle light on the broken places—the hidden cracks, the wounds that have quietly influenced your decisions, your patterns, and even the way you see yourself. This process isn't about judgment; it's about awareness. Because what remains hidden cannot be healed. But the work doesn't stop there. A good counselor doesn't leave you standing in the rubble of what's broken. They walk beside you, step by step, showing you a way out. The journey may take courage, but it isn't traveled alone. Their role is not just to diagnose but to guide, not just to reveal pain but to offer hope. Counseling, at its best, is an act of both truth and compassion. It honors your story, respects your faith, and points you toward a path where healing is possible. And as you walk that path, you discover that wholeness isn't the absence of brokenness—it's the transformation of it.

On the Other Side of Fear is Your Freedom

Trigger Warning — Please Read Before Moving Further
This portion of the chapter includes a first-person account of a severe spiritual attack that includes intrusive suicidal thoughts and intense emotional distress. If you have experienced similar moments, the material may be upsetting or triggering. Please care for yourself: stop reading if you feel overwhelmed, read later when you are with a trusted person, or skip the remainder of this chapter altogether.

If you are in immediate danger or feel you might harm yourself or someone else, get help right now.

- In the United States: **Call or text 988** or dial **911**.
- If you are outside the U.S.: contact your local emergency number or search for your country's crisis/suicide hotline online and call that number immediately.

If you are not in immediate danger but need support, consider these next steps:

- Call a trusted friend, spouse/partner, family member, pastor, or spiritual leader and tell them what you're feeling. Ask them to stay with you or to come quickly.
- Contact a mental health professional (therapist, counselor, psychiatrist) and schedule an urgent appointment. If you do not have one, your primary care doctor can provide referrals.
- If you prefer crisis chat/text lines or online support, look up your local crisis line or community mental-health resources. Many countries have text/chat services and local hotlines.

- If you are in the U.S. and want ongoing community support, consider reaching out to organizations like NAMI (National Alliance on Mental Illness) for local resources and support groups.
- Remove or secure anything that could be used for self-harm if that is a concern in your home (medication, sharp objects,

---

On the Other Side of Fear is Your Freedom

firearms). Ask someone you trust to help with this if possible.

Practical immediate steps you can take if you feel overwhelmed but are not in immediate danger:

1. Put your feet on the floor and breathe: inhale for 4 counts, hold 4, exhale 6. Repeat until you feel a bit steadier.
2. Use a grounding exercise: name 5 things you can see, 4 things you can touch, 3 things you can hear, 2 things you can smell, 1 thing you can taste.
3. Call or text a trusted person and ask them to stay with you (on the phone or in person). Don't be alone.
4. Pray or read a short Scripture you know (see Prayer below). Speak it aloud if you can.
5. If suicidal thoughts persist or grow stronger, call emergency services or a crisis line immediately.

This portion of the chapter is written to encourage and to testify of God's deliverance. It is not a substitute for professional mental-health care. If the material raises unresolved pain or risk, please seek professional and spiritual help right away.

On the Other Side of Fear is Your Freedom

A Morning I Will Never Forget

It happened one morning—and some will believe me and some won't, but I'm going to tell you anyway. I got up and went into my husband's man-cave, the quiet place where I often pray and start my day. As I almost reached the door, a voice cut through the silence like a knife: "You are going to kill your kids and then you are going to kill yourself." I don't know how to describe that moment except to say the air changed. I immediately said out loud, "no I'm not." The voice snapped back, "Yes, you are!" Fear poured through me. I woke one of my daughters and asked her to pray with me. She sat with me, holding me as I cried out to God, but the voice grew louder and angrier and it was hard to focus. Then, as if from far away and somehow very near at once, I heard a still, small voice say, "Go get in your shower." I left my daughter praying in the room and obeyed. I got into the shower, and almost immediately the murderous voice stopped. In that small, steamy space I felt a break in the darkness. For a brief moment I could breathe. I often pray in my shower. When I got out, the voice returned. Terrified, I called my husband and begged him to come home. I called family and a bishop, and I even reached out to the suicide hotline. People prayed with me—my husband, my bishop, my first lady, others—and I am grateful for every voice lifted on my behalf. Still, the heaviness didn't fully shift. A sister in Christ I had been spending time praying with answered when I told her what had happened and she said, "Let's pray." I don't know why the previous prayers didn't bring the same breakthrough, but when she prayed, something broke in the atmosphere—and just like that, it was gone. I had never encountered a spirit that strong. Even though I know the Word of God, I needed reinforcements. If your case ever feels as severe as this—if voices tell you to harm yourself or others, or if you feel in danger—please seek help immediately. Do not let it linger. Call emergency services, go to the nearest hospital, contact a trusted pastor or spiritual leader, and call your local crisis line. In the United States you can call or text **988** for the Suicide & Crisis Lifeline. If any children are in danger, call emergency services right away.

On the Other Side of Fear is Your Freedom

Short Devotional — "When You Feel Attacked"

A brief practice to use when fear, dark thoughts, or voices come (Use wherever you are—say it out loud if you can. If you can't speak aloud, whisper or say these words in your heart.)

1. **Pause and breathe.** Sit or stand. Breathe slowly: in for 4, hold 4, out for 6. Tell your body you are safe for this moment.

2. **Declare God's presence.** Out loud (or in your spirit) say: "God is here. The Lord is with me" *(NKJV, Psalm 46:1; Psalm 34:18).*

3. **Call for help.** If possible, call a trusted person: spouse, friend, pastor, family member—ask them to pray and to stay with you. If you feel unsafe, call emergency services or your local crisis number now.

4. **Pray this short prayer:** *"Heavenly Father, I am afraid and I don't want these thoughts. I ask You to surround me with Your peace. Send Your Spirit now. Silence every lying voice. Strengthen me with Your truth and with people who will stand with me. In Jesus' name, Amen."*

5. **Speak Scripture over the moment:**
   - "The Lord is near to those who have a broken heart" *(NKJV, Psalm 34:18).*
   - "Greater is He that is in you than he that is in the world" *(KJV 1 John 4:4).*
   - "Be anxious for nothing; in everything, by prayer and supplication, with thanksgiving, let your requests be made known to God; and the peace of God which surpasses all understanding will guard your heart and mind" *(NKJV, Philippians 4:6–7).*

On the Other Side of Fear is Your Freedom

6. **Move to safety and company.** If you can, go to a place where someone you trust is present. If you're alone, call a crisis line or emergency services.

Closing Encouragement

You don't have to face the darkness alone. God hears you. People can and will help you if you tell them. If you ever feel unsafe, act immediately — call 988 (U.S.), your local emergency number, or a crisis line where you live. You are precious and loved, and help is available.

On the Other Side of Fear is Your Freedom

CHAPTER Six

Fearless and Afraid

I'll never forget my first experience with bullying. Terrified to say anything back, scared to fight, I just took the abuse. It started in 3rd grade and lasted all the way through my senior year in high school. It felt like I was a magnet for bullies. The faces changed, but the spirit was the same. I had these big ol' buck teeth that took me years to grow into, so I was an easy target. And it wasn't just strangers or kids I didn't know—many of my own family members joined in. I never stood up, and I never fought back. For years, fear owned me. Ten long years passed before I finally found the courage to be brave. It was my senior year of high school when a girl confronted me because someone told her I said something terrible about her baby. It was a lie, just an excuse to come after me. She caught me in the stairwell with my arms full of books. My heart was racing, but before she could make a move, I swung on her first. My books went flying everywhere. The next thing I remember was being on the ground, kicked by several of her friends. No, I didn't win that fight. But I did win the war. I know what you're probably thinking: How? You totally got your butt kicked. And I did. But here's why I won the war—I conquered fear. For the first time, I stood up for myself. I didn't let fear keep me down, silence me, or own me anymore. And after that day, they never messed with me again. Fighting with your fists is a terrible way to deal with fear, so please understand that I am not endorsing or condoning physical fighting. What I hope you see is that the real fight wasn't with that girl in the stairwell. The true battle was happening on the inside of me. She just happened to be the face of fear that day. All those years of silence, of shrinking back, of letting fear run my life had built up to that moment. When I finally swung, it wasn't really at her—it was at the fear that had controlled me for so long. Looking back, I wish I had stood up sooner. All those years of hiding, of living in turmoil, could have been different if I had only faced fear head-on. Maybe if I had dealt with fear earlier, anxiety wouldn't have found its way into my life years later. Who knows? But one thing I do know for sure is this: fear was defeated then, and its defeated now. Fear is tricky because it doesn't live outside of us—it lives inside. It takes root in the mind and works against your body from the inside out. As long as you stay afraid, fear gives birth to anxiety and wreaks havoc in every part of your life. But when you decide to stand tall, to turn around and face it—not in your own strength, but with the living God inside of you and standing beside you—fear loses all its power. This reminds me of David when he faced Goliath *(Holy Bible, KJV, 2017, 1Samuel 17:1-51)*. To everyone watching, David didn't look like he stood a chance. Goliath was bigger, stronger, and armed with weapons David didn't have. Just like me standing in that stairwell, David seemed outnumbered and outmatched. But the real battle wasn't about size or strength—it was about fear. The entire Israelite army had been paralyzed by it, but David refused to let fear win. He didn't fight in his own ability; he fought in the name of the Lord. And that was enough. That day in the stairwell may not have looked like victory to anyone else, but for me, it was the beginning of learning how to fight back. Just as David ran toward his giant with faith, I faced mine—and fear lost its grip. Every time anxiety tries to creep back into my life, I remember this truth: the same God who gave David victory over Goliath, and gave me courage to stand up for myself, is the same God

---

On the Other Side of Fear is Your Freedom

who fights for me and you today. God's Word will drive you to press forward, just as it drove David to press through when he faced Goliath. We all have giants in our lives, and anxiety is just one of them. Giants come in many forms—fear, doubt, grief, shame, loss, insecurity—and each one stands tall, trying to intimidate us into backing down. But just as David stood before Goliath with nothing but a sling, a stone, and unshakable faith, you too can face the giants in your life with the Word of God as your weapon. David didn't win the battle because he was stronger or more experienced—he won because he trusted God to fight for him. Everyone around him thought he was unqualified and too small. His own brothers doubted him, King Saul tried to dress him in armor that didn't fit, and Goliath mocked him to his face. Yet David refused to put his confidence in himself. He declared boldly in 1 Samuel 17:45: "... You come against me with sword and spear and javelin, but I come against you in the name of the Lord Almighty..."*(Holy Bible, NIV, 2011, 1Samuel 17:45)*. That's what gave him victory. Anxiety is a giant that looks impossible to defeat. It mocks you, it looms over you, and it tells you that you'll never win. But like David, you don't need to rely on human strength or conventional weapons. You don't need to have it all figured out. What you need is faith—faith that God is bigger than your giant. His Word is your stone, and His presence is your strength. Every time you declare His promises over your life, you are aiming your sling at the forehead of fear. This journey of slaying giants looks different for everyone. Some of you will grab hold of these truths and experience breakthrough quickly—you were ready to receive, and deliverance will come like David's stone, knocking your giant down in one strike. Others may find the process slower. You may start strong, stumble, and feel like you're beginning again. But hear me: that's okay. David didn't become a giant-slayer overnight—he spent years in the fields, fighting lions and bears, building his faith one battle at a time. Each of those smaller victories prepared him for the day he stood before Goliath. Your story is no different. Every struggle you've overcome has prepared you for this moment. You've slain many giants before, and you will

---

On the Other Side of Fear is Your Freedom

slay many more in the future. Even when the battle feels long, every step forward is proof that God is at work in you—physically, mentally, emotionally, and spiritually. The beautiful truth is this: you are not fighting alone. The God who gave David victory is the same God who stands beside you today. And just as David ran toward his giant instead of away from it, you too can press forward, knowing that God is with you, guiding your aim, and ensuring that the giant before you will fall.

At first glance, the chapter title "Fearless and Afraid" may sound contradictory, but it perfectly describes the tension of living with anxiety while holding onto faith. How can you be both at the same time? Yet this is exactly what it feels like to walk through the battle with anxiety. On one hand, you have the truth of God's Word reminding you over and over: "Fear not, for I am with you..."(Holy Bible, NKJV, 1982, Isaiah 41:10). You know in your heart that God is your protector, your comforter, and your peace. That knowledge gives you a fearless spirit. But on the other hand, your body doesn't always get the memo. Your palms sweat, your chest tightens, your thoughts race—and the fear feels real. Being *"fearless"* doesn't mean you never feel fear. It means you refuse to let fear dictate your actions or rob you of the promises God has spoken over your life. It means that even when anxiety shows up pounding on the door of your heart, you answer it with faith. Fear may whisper, *"You can't handle this."* But faith responds, "God is our refuge and strength, a very present help in trouble"(Holy Bible, KJV, 2017, Psalm 46:1). Fear tries to convince you that the panic won't pass, that the storm will never end. Faith counters with, "Peace I leave with you, my peace I give unto you.."(KJV, John 14:27). In those moments, you might feel both fearless and afraid at the same time. Fearful in your humanity, yet fearless in your spirit. That tension is where God's strength becomes most visible. Paul reminds us in 2 Corinthians 12:9, that God's power is made perfect in our weakness *(KJV, 2Corithians 12:9)*. That means it's not about pretending the fear doesn't exist—it's about acknowledging it while still standing firm in the truth that you are never fighting

---

On the Other Side of Fear is Your Freedom

alone. When you embrace this paradox, you free yourself from shame. Too often, we beat ourselves up for "still being afraid," thinking it means our faith is weak. But the opposite is true: faith is choosing to trust God despite the fear. It's walking forward with shaky legs and a racing heart, because deep down you know God's hand is holding you steady. That's what it means to be fearless and afraid. It's not denial. It's not weakness. It's victory in motion. Fear may show up, but it cannot win. When you begin applying the principles in this book to your life, anxiety will leave you for a season. You will feel things returning to normal, and slowly you will begin to find your footing again. As intrusive thoughts come your way, your spiritual shield of faith will fend off the darts of the enemy's attack. You will feel strong, powerful, and victorious over anxiety. And in that season, you truly are. But don't be surprised when anxiety tries to return. Your body has been trained over time to respond in certain ways, and in a moment of weakness—when you haven't prayed, or when your defenses are down—the enemy will strike.

Again, you will be tempted to allow anxiety back into your life—to settle for coping instead of conquering. But that is not the life God promised you. You deserve to live in the fullness of His promises, not below your inherited rights and privileges as His child. It takes courage to overcome anxiety. You live in a world where many people don't truly understand what it even is, yet you face it head-on every single day while still trying to live what looks like a normal life. The truth is, anxiety alters you in ways that force you to discover a new normal. Things may never go back to the way they were, but they can and will become better. There is something innate in us that craves comfort and wants to return to what feels familiar, even if it isn't good for us. But progress doesn't come through comfort—it takes work, it takes action, and it most certainly takes faith. "Without faith it is impossible to please God" (Hebrews 11:6). Each day, show God that you trust Him. Show Him that you take Him at His Word. Let your life declare that you believe He has your best interests at heart, and that He will perfect all that concerns you. And as you

---

On the Other Side of Fear is Your Freedom

walk in that kind of faith, watch how God rewards your faithfulness with strength, peace, and victory.

Reflection Pause
Write down your answers honestly. Remember—faith is built step by step, choice by choice, and God honors every effort you make to trust Him.

- In what ways have you been tempted to *"just cope"* with anxiety instead of conquering it?
- What does your *"new normal"* look like, and how can you invite God into it each day?
- What step of faith can you take today to show God that you trust Him at His Word?

Prayer
Heavenly Father, I thank You that You have not given me a spirit of fear, but of power, love, and a sound mind. Forgive me for the times I have settled for coping instead of conquering. Today, I choose to trust You with my whole heart. I believe Your Word is true, and I declare that You are perfecting all that concerns me. Strengthen me to walk boldly in faith, even when I feel weak. Thank You for fighting my battles and for giving me peace that the world cannot take away. In Jesus' name, **Amen**.

Declarations

I will not live below my inheritance in Christ.

I will not just cope—I will conquer.

God is with me, God is for me, and His Word is my weapon.

Anxiety will not own me. I am free, I am strong, and I am an overcomer through Christ.

On the Other Side of Fear is Your Freedom

Trina Raeford

> "FOR WE WRESTLE NOT AGAINST FLESH AND BLOOD, BUT AGAINST PRINCIPALITIES, AGAINST POWERS, AGAINST THE RULERS OF THE DARKNESS OF THIS WORLD, AGAINST SPIRITUAL WICKEDNESS IN HIGH PLACES."
>
> EPHESIANS 6:12 KJV

CHAPTER
Seven

This Means War

You ever had someone mad at you, and for the life of you, you couldn't understand why? You find yourself playing out different scenarios, wondering if one of them is the reason, but you always come up short. Meanwhile, the person is rolling their eyes, snarling at you, cutting conversations short, or even standing and laughing with someone they know doesn't care for you. It's frustrating and confusing, because you're being treated like an enemy, but you can't figure out what you did to deserve it. That's how anxiety works too. It wages a secret war against you—often without your awareness. You don't remember inviting it in, yet suddenly it's rolling its eyes at your peace, snarling at your joy, cutting short your confidence, and cozying up with every lie the enemy has ever told you. You find yourself replaying moments, asking, *"What did I do wrong, why do I feel like this, and why can't I just shake it?"* You're under attack, but not in the way you think. Just like with that person's unexplained anger, anxiety isn't always about what's on the surface. It's about what's happening in the unseen spiritual realm—the spiritual war that's being waged against you. And unless you recognize it for what it is, you'll keep spinning in circles, trying to find answers in the wrong places. Anxiety is more than a feeling—it's a strategy of the enemy. And the first step to victory is naming it for what it really is: war. Anxiety doesn't knock on the door politely. Often, it shows up unannounced, slipping into your thoughts, your emotions, your body, until you realize you've been under attack without even knowing it. But make no mistake: anxiety is not just a mental or emotional struggle—it is a spiritual battle. "For we wrestle not against flesh and blood, but against principalities, against powers, against the rulers of the darkness of this world, against spiritual wickedness in high places"*(Holy Bible, KJV, 2017, Ephesians 6:12)*. If anxiety has declared war on your life, then you must rise up and declare war back—not in your own strength, but in the authority and power of Almighty God. Anxiety may use your mind and your emotions as its battlefield, but its true source is spiritual. That's why coping strategies alone never bring full freedom. You can soothe the symptoms, but unless you fight at the root, the war rages on. Anxiety wages war with stealth. It doesn't always show up with fanfare—it creeps in quietly, through subtle doubts, exhausting "what ifs," and paralyzing fears. One moment you're living life normally, and the next you feel as though the air has been sucked out of your lungs. You find yourself retreating into shadows, avoiding joy, and surrendering ground you didn't even realize you had. That's how anxiety works—by stealing, killing, and destroying in silence. If anxiety has declared war on you, you don't have to stand defenseless. You have access to the greatest weapons ever forged—the weapons of the Spirit. "For the weapons of our warfare are not carnal, but mighty through God to the pulling down of strongholds"*(KJV, 2Corinthians 10:4)*. Your fight is not with yourself. Your fight is with the forces of darkness that want to keep you bound. And God has already prepared you for battle. You don't walk into this war unarmed—you walk in clothed in the armor of God, backed by the authority of Jesus, and empowered by the Spirit who lives inside you. So yes, this means war. But war is not something to fear when you already know the outcome. The enemy has declared war on your peace, your joy, your future—but God has already declared your victory. The only question left is: will you pick up your weapons and fight? I'm not just talking about playing defense—that part is

---

On the Other Side of Fear is Your Freedom

easy. Anyone can throw up a shield and try to survive the blows. But God hasn't called you to simply survive—He's called you to overcome. The real question is: are you ready to go to the enemy's camp, fight on his turf, and take back what's yours? Because make no mistake, the enemy has stolen things from you—your peace, your joy, your confidence, your sleep, your boldness, your dreams. He's been trespassing on holy ground, and it's time you reminded him who you belong to. Scripture says,"The thief does not come except to steal, and to kill, and to destroy. I have come that they may have life, and that they may have it more abundantly"(Holy Bible, NKJV, 2017, John 10:10). The enemy's agenda is destruction. But Jesus already won the victory, and now He gives you the authority to enforce it. That means you don't just sit back and wait for the next attack, you take the fight to him. "And from the days of John the Baptist until now the kingdom of heaven suffers violence, and the violent take it by force"(NKJV, Matthew 11:12). This is not the time to be passive. This is the time to get violent in the Spirit—through prayer, through declaring God's Word, through worship, through fasting, through refusing to give up what God has promised you. So I'll ask you again: are you ready? Are you willing to rise up, armor on, sword in hand, and march into the enemy's camp to reclaim every blessing, every promise, and every victory that belongs to you? You have been trying to fight anxiety in your flesh—and you keep losing. You've tried willpower, positive thinking, distractions, even numbing the pain with busyness or unhealthy habits. You're putting up a fight, but anxiety keeps returning no matter how hard you fight. And yet, the cycle continues. Why? Because you can't defeat a spiritual enemy with fleshly weapons. If this is happening to you, it is time to check what's in your arsenal. If sin is in your arsenal, then you are defeated before you even begin. You cannot fight a victorious battle while holding on to the very thing that empowers your enemy. We all sin and fall short of the glory of God (NKJV, Romans 3:23), but what I am talking about here is habitual sin—the kind you've excused, justified, or hidden. Habitual sin weakens your spirit, disarms your weapons, clouds your discernment, and drains

On the Other Side of Fear is Your Freedom

your confidence in prayer. Worst of all, it creates an opening in your armor where the enemy can strike. You cannot walk in authority over anxiety, fear, or any other attack when you are still bowing to sin behind closed doors. Hebrews 12:1 tells us to "...lay aside every weight, and the sin which so easily ensnares us, and let us run with endurance the race that is set before us" *(NKJV, Hebrews 12:1)*. Habitual sin is that weight. It slows you down, keeps you bound, and leaves you vulnerable on the battlefield. Sin doesn't have to remain in your arsenal. Through confession, repentance, and the power of the Holy Spirit, you can lay it down. "If we confess our sins, He is faithful and just to forgive us our sins and to cleanse us from all unrighteousness"*(NKJV, 1John 1:9)*. Freedom begins the moment you stop protecting sin and start surrendering it. Anxiety already declares war on your peace—you cannot afford to give it extra ammunition. Purity, submission, and repentance strengthen your arsenal. Hidden sin weakens it. The choice is yours: will you carry a weapon that empowers your enemy, or will you lay it down so God can equip you with weapons that truly win? Submission to God must also be in your arsenal before we can even begin to discuss weapons. Without submission, every other tool you try to use in battle will fail. You can't wield the sword of the Spirit with power if you're still fighting God's authority. You can't lift the shield of faith with confidence if your life is out of alignment with His Word. Without submission, every other weapon you carry is weakened. You can know Scripture, quote affirmations, even pray—but if your life is not surrendered to God, you're swinging a dull sword. The enemy recognizes authority, and authority only comes from alignment with the Father. James 4:7 gives us the blueprint: "Therefore submit to God. Resist the devil and he will flee from you"*(NKJV, James 4:7)*. Notice that submission comes first. Too often, we try to resist the devil in our own strength. We grit our teeth, we try harder, we push back against anxiety, temptation, or fear—but nothing changes. Why? Because resistance without submission has no power. You cannot resist the devil or any of his vices—like anxiety—until you've surrendered yourself to God first. Submission is not weakness—it's alignment. When

---

On the Other Side of Fear is Your Freedom

you submit to God, you are placing yourself under His covering. You are saying, *"Lord, I can't win this battle in my own strength, but I align myself with Your will, Your Word, and Your way."* And it is in that posture that resistance becomes effective. That is when the enemy flees—not because of who you are, but because of whose authority you stand in. Submission is not a passive weapon—it's an offensive one. It positions you for victory. It puts you in step with God's Spirit, so every word you speak, every prayer you pray, and every truth you declare carries divine weight. If submission is missing from your arsenal, you will keep fighting in your flesh—and you will keep losing. But once you surrender, you fight clothed in God's strength, and the enemy cannot stand against that. So if anxiety has been holding you hostage, check your arsenal. Have you submitted fully to God? Because once you do, your resistance gains authority—and the enemy has no choice but to flee. The next weapon in your arsenal is walking in the Spirit. Once you've submitted yourself to God, the Spirit becomes your guide, your strength, and your vision. Without Him, you are fighting blind. With Him, the unseen realm becomes visible, and suddenly you recognize what you're truly up against. Paul reminds us in Galatians 5:16, *"So I say, walk by the Spirit, and you will not gratify the desires of the flesh"(Holy Bible, NIV, 2011, Galatians 5:16).* Walking in the Spirit isn't just about resisting temptation—it's about seeing with spiritual eyes. What looks like constant worry may actually be an attack of fear. What looks like rejection may actually be a spirit of intimidation. What looks like depression may be a spirit of heaviness. When you walk in the Spirit, the lies of the enemy are exposed for what they are. The Spirit not only reveals the battle, He empowers you to fight. Jesus called Him "the Spirit of Truth" who guides us into all truth *(NKJV, John 16:13).* That means when anxiety tries to feed you lies, the Spirit is the voice inside that says, *"No, that's not who you are. This is what God says about you."* Walking in the Spirit is like having night vision on the battlefield. Everyone else may stumble in the dark, swinging at shadows, but you can see the enemy clearly—and more importantly, you can see the path to victory.

On the Other Side of Fear is Your Freedom

At first, *"walking in the Spirit"* can sound complicated—like it's reserved for people who are more spiritual or holier than you. But the truth is, walking in the Spirit is not about perfection; it's about direction. It simply means living your life led by God's Spirit instead of being driven by your flesh.

Here are some practical ways to walk in the Spirit:

1. Start with Surrender.
Every day, begin by inviting the Holy Spirit to lead you. It can be as simple as praying, *"Holy Spirit, guide my thoughts, words, and actions today"* (NKJV, Romans 8:14). That daily surrender sets the tone.

2. Stay in the Word.
The Spirit speaks most clearly through God's Word. The more Scripture you read and meditate on, the more the Spirit has to bring to your remembrance when anxiety or lies try to creep in (NKJV, John 14:26).

3. Pray Continually.
Prayer isn't just a once-a-day ritual; it's a constant conversation. As you go through your day, ask the Spirit questions, thank Him for small victories, and listen for His promptings *(NIV, 1Thessalonians 5:17)*.

4. Obey Quickly.
The Spirit will nudge you—sometimes gently, sometimes firmly. When He tells you to let go of something, speak to someone, or step into an opportunity, obey. Delayed obedience is disobedience *(NKJV, Galatians 5:25)*.

5. Guard Your Atmosphere.

Walking in the Spirit means being mindful of what you feed your soul—what you watch, listen to, and entertain. The Spirit thrives in an atmosphere of worship, truth, and purity *(NKJV, Philippians 4:8)*. Walking in the Spirit is not about trying harder—it's about leaning closer. It's not a one-time event; it's a lifestyle of letting God lead. And when you do, you begin to see with clarity. The unseen realm becomes visible. The lies lose their power. And you fight not in confusion, but in confidence.

Weapons of the Spirit

Once you've surrendered to God, removed the foothold of sin, and chosen to walk in the Spirit, you are equipped to use God's weapons of warfare.. God has not left you vulnerable or unequipped. He has placed powerful weapons in your hands—divine weapons that can tear down strongholds, silence the lies of the enemy, and defeat the spirit of anxiety at its root. With submission as your covering, the Spirit as your guide, and a life of holiness as your strength, you step onto the battlefield not as a victim but as a victor.

• The Word of God (Your Sword)

The Word is your most powerful weapon. Ephesians 6:17 calls it "the sword of the Spirit"*(NIV, Ephesians 6:17)*. When anxiety attacks, you must speak God's promises out loud. Don't just think them—declare them boldly. Jesus Himself defeated Satan in the wilderness by quoting scripture. If the Son of God fought with the Word, so must we.

On the Other Side of Fear is Your Freedom

- **Prayer (Your Lifeline)**

Prayer is not just asking God for things—it is communion with Him. It realigns your heart with His and keeps you sensitive to the Spirit. Prayer keeps your armor strong. When you feel anxiety pressing in, pray without hesitation. Call on His name, and He will draw near.

- **Worship (Your Atmosphere Shifter)**

Worship confuses the enemy. When you praise God in the middle of anxiety, you shift your focus off the fear and onto the One who has power over it. Worship invites God's presence into your situation, and where His presence is, fear cannot stay.

- **Fasting (Your Spiritual Reset)**

Fasting crucifies the flesh and sharpens your spirit. It helps break unhealthy attachments and makes you more sensitive to the voice of God. If anxiety has had a stronghold in your life, fasting can be a powerful key to breaking chains.

- **Community (Your Support)**

God never designed you to fight alone. Surround yourself with people of faith—trusted friends, counselors, or a church family—who will pray for you, encourage you, and remind you of the truth when you forget. This is not weakness; it is wisdom. Even David had mighty men to stand with him in battle.

- **The Shield of Faith (Your Defense)**

Faith is what extinguishes the fiery darts of the enemy (NKJV, Ephesians 6:16). When anxiety throws lies at you—*"you're not strong enough," "you'll never be*

On the Other Side of Fear is Your Freedom

free," "this will never end"—you raise the shield of faith and declare, "God's Word says otherwise." Faith doesn't deny the reality of fear; it declares a greater reality: God is with me.

These are not temporary fixes—they are eternal tools. God's weapons of warfare are not like bandages that cover wounds for a season; they are everlasting instruments of victory that dismantle strongholds and silence the enemy. Pick them up daily. Use them with boldness. Stand firm, knowing that every swing of the sword, every prayer lifted, every word of truth declared carries the power of heaven behind it. And never forget this: the battle is not yours, but the Lord's *(NKJV, 2Chronicles 20:15)*. You are not fighting for victory—you are fighting from victory. Jesus has already overcome, and because you belong to Him, that victory is your inheritance. Anxiety may roar, the enemy may attack, but their defeat is already sealed. So step forward with courage. Live with your weapons in hand. And remember, when you fight God's way, you never fight alone—and you never fight in vain.

On the Other Side of Fear is Your Freedom

CHAPTER
Eight

> Overcomer

I have always loved movies that celebrate triumph—stories where a character faces impossible odds, pushes through the pain, and emerges victorious. Boxing movies like Rocky have always resonated with me. In those films, the characters were surrounded by reasons to quit. The world told them they didn't stand a chance. They could have chosen a life of mediocrity and still survived. But the champion inside of them wouldn't allow it. Something deep within demanded more. That same spirit of triumph lives in us. Muhammad Ali captured it perfectly when he declared, *"I am the greatest. I said that even before I knew I was."* There is something profoundly spiritual happening in that statement. It is both an affirmation and a manifestation. Long before the world recognized his greatness, Ali spoke it into existence. Scripture confirms this truth. The Word of God tells us to *"call those things which do not exist as though they did"*(Holy Bible, NKJV, 1982, Romans 4:17). We are not just flesh and blood—we are spirits possessing a body, and we have a soul (NKJV, 1Thessalonians 5:23). And the Bible reminds us, *"Death and life are in the power of the tongue, and those who love it will eat its fruit"(NKJV, Proverbs 18:21).* What we think is powerful, yes—but what we speak carries the authority to create, to shape, and to transform reality. When we understand this, we begin to see that speaking life, truth, and destiny isn't just positive thinking. It's a spiritual act. As children of God, we carry His nature within us. Just as He spoke the universe into being *(Holy Bible, NIV, 2011, Genesis 1:3)*, we too have been given the power to call forth what is unseen *(NIV, 2 Corinthians 4:13)*. Our words carry weight in the spiritual realm. They can tear down or build up, curse or bless, limit or liberate *(NIV, James 3:9-10)*. That's why mediocrity is never the final word for those who belong to Christ. The champion within you won't let you settle. You may be in the fight of your life, but victory is already written in your DNA: "But thanks be to God, who gives us the victory through our Lord Jesus Christ" *(NIV, 1 Corinthians 15:57)*. Your thoughts fuel the battle, but your words—spoken in faith—swing the knockout punch. An overcomer isn't someone who never faces challenges or adversity. An overcomer is someone who refuses to give up—no matter how many times life knocks them down. They keep rising, even when every part of them aches and getting up feels gut-wrenching. The victory in their triumph always outweighs the pain of standing again. Some of us don't even fully understand why we keep getting back up. But if you are a believer, it is because the Spirit of God lives within you. That power fuels you toward victory *(NIV, 1 John 5:4)*. Failure may trip you, hardship may wound you, but defeat cannot define you. I know this truth personally. I have failed many times. I've walked through seasons of homelessness and despair, pregnant and going from couch to couch just trying to survive. And yet here I am, writing these words to you. Where would my life be if I had chosen to stay down? If I had accepted the lie that failure was final? The Word tells us, "The righteous may fall seven times and rise again" *(NIV, Proverbs 24:16)*. God has placed within you the strength to endure. His promise is sure: "No temptation has overtaken you except such as is common to man; but God is faithful, who will not allow you to be tempted beyond what you are able, but with the temptation will also make the way of escape, that you may be able to bear it" *(NKJV, 1 Corinthians 10:13)*. That means God knew you could survive it. He knew you could come out of it stronger. He knew you

---

On the Other Side of Fear is Your Freedom

could learn from it. And He knew your story could help someone else who might not yet see their own strength. You are not still standing because of luck. You are standing because you are chosen. Because you are more than a conqueror through Christ (NKJV, Romans 8:37). I remember asking myself over and over again: Why wasn't I strong enough to deal with anxiety? Why did it choose me? What did I do so differently from other people who grieve and go through hardship? Those questions haunted me. They made me feel weak, singled out, even punished. But over time, I realized something: anxiety doesn't mean you are weak. Struggle doesn't mean you are less than. Pain is not evidence of failure. In fact, some of the strongest people I've ever known have fought invisible battles daily and still chose to keep going. Jesus Himself reminded us that "in this world you will have trouble"(NIV, John 16:33). Struggle isn't a matter of if—it's a matter of when. But He didn't stop there. He finished that promise with hope: "But take heart! I have overcome the world" (NIV, John 16:33). Anxiety, grief, trials—none of these are proof that you are defective. They are simply reminders that you are human, living in a broken world, and in need of a Savior who promises to walk with you through it. Scripture says, "My grace is sufficient for you, for my power is made perfect in weakness" (NKJV 2 Corinthians 12:9). What if the very place you feel weakest is the place where His strength wants to show up the most? So maybe the real question isn't *"Why me?"* but *"What now?"* Instead of wondering why, you can start to ask how God wants to use it. Because even anxiety can become a testimony of resilience, faith, and victory when you keep walking—step by step—with Him. You may not be able to control the battles you face, but you can decide how you respond to them. Life will hand you struggles you didn't ask for, and sometimes you'll carry weights you never thought you could bear. But the real measure of an overcomer isn't found in avoiding the fire—it's found in walking through it with purpose. When you ask, *"What now?"* you're shifting your focus from the pain to the possibility. You're choosing to see beyond the anxiety, the grief, or the setback, and instead asking: What can God do with this? How can He use

On the Other Side of Fear is Your Freedom

this part of my story? Who might be encouraged if I don't give up here? The Word tells us, "And we know that all things work together for good to those who love God, to those who are the called according to His purpose"*(NKJV, Romans 8:28)*. That doesn't mean every circumstance is good. But it does mean that God is able to weave even the hardest moments into something redemptive. So the answer to *"What now?"* is not despair—it's decision. Decide to rise again. Decide to let your story be fuel for someone else's faith. Decide to believe that what the enemy meant for harm, God will turn for good (NKJV, Genesis 50:20). Your *"what now"* moment is where transformation begins. It's where you step out of the shadow of why and into the light of what's next.

What's Next?

This is the question of vision. It's no longer about looking back at what hurt you, or even just surviving the moment you're in—it's about stepping into the future God has prepared for you. Scripture says, "For I know the plans I have for you," declares the Lord, "plans to prosper you and not to harm you, plans to give you a hope and a future"*(NKJV, Jeremiah 29:11)*. Asking *"What's next?"* positions your heart to see beyond the ashes and into the promise. What's next might not look like a giant leap—it may be one small step of faith at a time. It might be choosing to go back to therapy, to forgive someone who hurt you, to apply for the job, to write the book, or simply to believe again. Every step matters because it moves you closer to who God designed you to be. The Apostle Paul said it this way: "... Forgetting those things which are behind and reaching forward to those things which are ahead, I press toward the goal for the prize of the upward call of God in Christ Jesus"*(NKJV, Philippians 3:13-14)*. What's next is about pressing forward. It's about refusing to stay stuck in what was, and instead daring to live in what can be. So, what's next for you? It's not just survival—it's significance. It's not just getting through—it's rising up. It's not just about your healing—it's about the lives your story will touch when you share it.

On the Other Side of Fear is Your Freedom

What is an Overcomer?

An overcomer is dripping in victory even when they cannot see it. Victory is not only in the moment of the win—it's in every step that leads up to it. It's in the choice to rise again after failure. It's in the decision to keep moving when everything inside you says to quit. It's in the quiet prayers whispered through tears, the faith that refuses to die, and the courage to take one more step. Sometimes victory is invisible to the natural eye, but it is no less real. The Word tells us, "For we walk by faith, not by sight" *(NKJV, 2Corinthians 5:7)*. That means your triumph is not determined by what you can see right now but by what God has already declared over your life. You may feel broken, exhausted, or unsure—but in Christ, you are already more than a conqueror *(NKJV, Romans 8:37)*. To be an overcomer is to carry victory in your very being, long before it shows up in your circumstances. It's to know that the crown is already yours, even when you are still in the middle of the fight. So even if you don't see it today, wear your victory. Walk in it. Drip in it. Because heaven has already declared: "Thanks be to God, who gives us the victory through our Lord Jesus Christ" *(NIV, 1Corinthians 15:57)*. You are an overcomer! How do I know it? The very fact that you picked up this book is enough for me to know. Something inside of you refuses to give up. Something within you believes that there is more to your story than what you've been through. That spark—that decision to reach for help, for truth, for hope—is the evidence that you are already overcoming. Being an overcomer doesn't mean you never fall, never hurt, or never question. It means you keep moving anyway. It means that when life knocks you down, you rise again. It means that even with shaky hands, tear-filled eyes, or a heart heavy with grief, you still choose to turn the page. That choice, simple as it seems, is powerful. The Bible declares, "For whatever is born of God overcomes the world. And this is the victory that has overcome the world—our faith" *(NIV 1John 5:4)*. That's why I can say with full confidence: you are an overcomer. It isn't just about what you've done—it's about who you are in Christ. So, as you read these words, know this: you're not here by accident. God has

---

On the Other Side of Fear is Your Freedom

led you to this moment because He knows you're ready. Ready to believe again. Ready to fight again. Ready to walk in the victory that's already yours. The signs were always there. You may not have noticed them in the moment, but they've been etched into your journey all along. You keep getting back up. You survived what should have broken you. You choose faith over fear. You've turned pain into purpose. You refuse to settle for mediocrity. You still believe in your future. And through it all, you've known—sometimes quietly, sometimes boldly—that your victory comes from Christ. You don't have to wonder if you are an overcomer. The evidence is written in your resilience, your faith, your persistence, and your hope. Every scar, every battle, every comeback has testified to who you really are. Scripture says, "In all these things we are more than conquerors through Him who loved us" (NIV, Romans 8:37). That means you weren't just surviving—you were overcoming the whole time. And now, as you recognize the signs, you can walk in confidence, knowing that the champion inside of you has been alive all along. Anxiety wanted me to keep this journey quiet. It whispered that I should stay in the shadows, that my story was too messy, too embarrassing to share. It told me no one would care, and no one would ever read it. That's how the enemy works—he thrives in silence, hoping that shame will keep us bound. But God works differently. Sometimes He gives you a glimpse of what's to come, just enough to remind you that He's still writing your story. For me, that glimpse came when I met a wonderful group of women who were excited about the idea of this book—even before a single word was written. They believed in the vision without needing to see the content. That was God's way of reminding me: *"You are not alone, and what I've placed in you matters."* God is wonderful like that. He knows how to send encouragement at the exact moment you need it. He gave me the courage to finally do what I had always longed to do: write a book. And what better way to fulfill that dream than to pour my words into something that could help someone else—someone who feels the same shadows I once felt, someone who needs to know they are not alone. This book is more than pages—it is a testimony, a lifeline, and an act

---

On the Other Side of Fear is Your Freedom

of obedience. And if even one person finds hope through these words, then every battle, every whisper of anxiety, and every moment of doubt will have been worth it.

This Book Right Here

Writing this book is one of the hardest things I have ever done. Somehow, I always end up doing the hard things. And yet, this one feels different—because it carries so much weight, so much love, so much purpose. I wish my sister were here to see this moment. If she were, she would have been the first to buy this book, the first to show it off, the first to cheer me on and tell me how proud she was. I wanted her to have more time—to live out her greatness, to finally see how good life could be for her. She deserved that. She struggled so much. But now she is in the best place of all—safe with our Father in Heaven. She was always helping people, always pouring herself out. And maybe that's why this book feels like my love letter—not only to her, but to you, and to everyone who has ever struggled with anxiety, with feelings of not being enough, or with doubts about what they could achieve. My husband was right when he told me this book would be therapy for me. With every story I shared, I relived the pain, the lessons, and the victories. Not to dwell on them, but so that you could have the help and encouragement you need and deserve. This was never just about me—it was always about you too. Anxiety tried to creep in during the writing. He tried to silence me, distract me, convince me this book would never be finished. Why? Because he knows knowledge is power. He knows the lives that will be touched, delivered, and set free by these pages. He knows that every word of truth you've read has become a weapon in your hands, and he knows his time is short. We have overcome anxiety—not by our own strength, not by quick fixes, not by coping—but by standing on the Word of God. "For whatever is born of God overcomes the world. And this is the victory that has overcome the world—our faith"(NIV, 1 John 5:4). Every truth you've read is now yours. Every scripture you've spoken is a stone in your sling. Every prayer you've

---

On the Other Side of Fear is Your Freedom

prayed has sharpened your sword. The enemy may come again, but you are no longer defenseless. You are trained. You are equipped. And you are covered by the presence of Almighty God. This book may end here, but your journey does not. Go forward in boldness, in courage, and in faith—knowing that the same God who carried me through will carry you too. You are more than a conqueror. You are free. You are strong. You are fearless. And this—this victory—**will forever be our legacy.**

On the Other Side of Fear is Your Freedom

If this book has touched your life in any way, I want to hear from you! Your story matters. Send your testimonies, questions, prayer requests, or reflections to **trina@anxietydefeated.com**. With your permission I may share excerpts (anonymously if you prefer) to encourage other readers. Thank you for letting me be a part of your journey; hearing how God moves through your life is one of the greatest joys of this work.

Consent line (copy this under the invitation if you'll publish stories): By submitting your testimony, you grant permission for the author to use excerpts in future editions, marketing, or related materials. Please state if you prefer your name withheld or details changed for privacy.

Stay Connected!
For more uplifting content and helpful resources, visit **www.anxietydefeated.com** and follow **@anxietydefeated** on all platforms!

References

American Psychological Association. (n.d.). *Anxiety*. In *APA dictionary of psychology*. Retrieved October 24, 2025, from https://dictionary.apa.org/anxiety

Fink, C. (2020, October 28). *Can we rewire our brains? Psychology Today*. https://www.psychologytoday.com/us/blog/changing-minds/202010/can-we-rewire-our-brains

Holy Bible, King James Version. (1769/2017). Cambridge University Press.

Holy Bible, New International Version. (2011). Zondervan.

Holy Bible, New King James Version. (1982). Thomas Nelson.

Psychology Today Staff. (n.d.). *Types of anxiety*. *Psychology Today*. https://www.psychologytoday.com/us/basics/anxiety/types-of-anxiety

Trina Raeford

Made in United States
Orlando, FL
05 December 2025